INTERMEDIATE

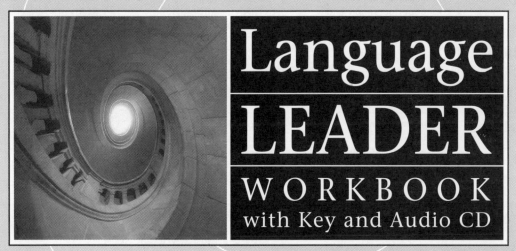

Language LEADER

WORKBOOK

with Key and Audio CD

PEARSON
Longman

John Hughes

CONTENTS

CONTENTS

1 Personality

1.1 PERSONALITY TYPES

VOCABULARY: personality adjectives

1 Underline the correct adjective in each sentence.

1 Jonathan is such a _sensible_/sensitive boy. He always does what the teacher asks and never gets into trouble.

2 He's so *adventurous/ambitious* that he said he intended to be the boss in two years time!

3 To avoid any mistakes, we need to be *serious/cautious* in a situation like this and not make decisions too quickly.

4 Be *energetic/assertive*! Make a decision and stick to it!

5 I like your new girlfriend. She's sociable without being too *talkative/easy-going*.

6 I think all older brothers tend to be quite *bossy/self-confident*. They usually tell their younger brothers what to do.

7 He isn't *energetic/creative* because of his father. It must be because of his mother. She was always making things or painting.

8 Introverts tend to be *organised/hard-working* in their approach – they like to know where everything is and make sure it goes back in its correct place.

PRONUNCIATION: word stress

2a `1.2` Listen and underline the main stress in each word.

1 ad<u>ven</u>turous	7 energetic
2 easy-<u>go</u>ing	8 organised
3 ambitious	9 reliable
4 even-tempered	10 self-confident
5 cautious	11 generous
6 open-minded	12 creative

2b `1.2` Now listen again and practise saying the words.

EXTRA VOCABULARY: negative prefixes

3 Match each prefix to an adjective to make it negative. Write it in a sentence 1–5.

	reliable
in	ambitious
im	sociable
un	patient
	sensitive

1 She's so _insensitive._ She should think before she speaks in case she hurts someone!

2 This job is really boring so let's employ someone who is _____ .

3 An _____ teacher is one who doesn't give students enough time to think.

4 I'm feeling rather _____ this evening. I don't think I'll go to the party.

5 I wouldn't expect him to arrive on time. He's fairly _____ .

TRANSLATION

4 How many of these adjectives can be directly translated into your language? What is the closest translation for the others?

1 sensitive _____

2 sensible _____

3 open-minded _____

4 hard-working _____

5 easy-going _____

6 moody _____

7 even-tempered _____

8 strong-willed _____

READING

Do you believe your handwriting can tell you about your personality? Take this test and find out!

1 Write your signature (or two words) in the square below.

2 Now answer these five questions about your handwriting. Tick (✔) answer a, b or c.

1 Does your handwriting

a) fill the box?

b) fill half the box?

c) fill a small part of the box?

2 Do the letters

a) point to the right?

b) go straight up and down?

c) point to the left?

3 Is there space between the two words?

a) No.

b) Not much.

c) Yes, a lot.

4 Did you underline the signature with

a) lots of lines?

b) one line?

c) no lines?

3 Count how many a, b or c answers you ticked. Then read below to find out what your score means.

Mostly As

You tend to be an extrovert. You like people to know you are in the room. You appear to be very ambitious and self-confident. You like to be where the action is and preferably to be in charge.

Mostly Bs

You can be sociable but you also like quiet times. You enjoy meeting people but there are only a few people you can call 'close friends'. You are hard-working but know how to relax and have fun.

Mostly Cs

You tend to prefer your own company or to have just a few close friends around for dinner instead of a large event. You can be ambitious but in general you don't make decisions quickly – you are cautious and when you speak, it's usually to make a thoughtful comment.

4 Use the handwriting test to analyse these signatures. Which signature shows the person is mostly a, b or c?

1

2

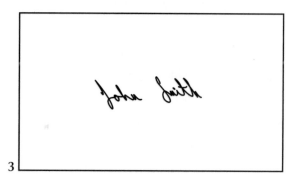

3

5 ▮1.3▮ A handwriting analyst is interpreting the signatures. Which signature is he describing, 1, 2 or 3?

DICTATION

LISTEN BETTER: dictations

When you first listen and write what you hear, you won't be able to write every word. Listen for the content words first of all, such as important verbs, adjectives or nouns. Then listen again and start to write the words in between, such as articles and pronouns.

6 `1.3` **Listen again and write in the missing parts.**

It obviously belongs to someone who walks into a room and likes everyone to know he's there. The way he uses the box tells me that _____

_____ . The signature looks fairly normal but the letters lean that way. If you combine that with the narrow gap between the words, then you have _____

and _____ .

Finally, the way he finishes off the signature with the lines makes _____

_____ .

GRAMMAR: question forms

7 **Write the missing question words in 1–8.**

Where	Does	Have	Is	How	Are
Do	What	Why	When		

1   _How_   reliable are the tests you use?

2   _____   exactly do psychiatrists do?

3   _____   you done any of these exercises?

4   _____   you ever get impatient?

5   _____   are you from?

6   _____   are you changing jobs?

7   _____   they living in Thailand now?

8   _____   he expect to be late?

9   _____   is Michael studying at the moment?

10   _____   long have you lived here?

11   _____   were you last in London?

12   _____   he easily annoyed?

8 **Complete these questions about Carl Jung.**

1   Who _was Carl Jung_____ ?

Carl Jung was a Swiss psychiatrist.

2   Where _____ ?

He studied medicine at the University of Basel.

3   What _____ ?

He specialised in psychiatric medicine.

4   What _____ ?

He developed ideas about personality types.

5   How many _____ ?

He identified two personality types.

6   Who _____ ?

Introverts don't like large crowds..

7   What _____ ?

Extroverts form close relationships.

8   How influential _____ ?

Jung was very influential.

9   Which _____ ?

The Myers-Briggs and Keirsey tests are based on his theory.

10   Which filmmaker _____ ?

Stanly Kubrick read his work..

11   What _____ ?

He tried to interpret dreams.

12   Which _____ ?

He wrote *The Undiscovered Self* in 1957.

VOCABULARY: prefixes

1 Write the correct missing prefix in sentences 1–8. Some of them are used more than once.

under-	dis-	ex-	mono-	mis-	~~anti-~~
over-	semi-	in-	bi-	re-	out-

1 I find him rather quiet and _anti_-social. When you try to start a conversation he walks away.

2 She's really _____ used at work. She wants more responsibility.

3 I saw your _____ girlfriend today. She was with a new man.

4 He's always been _____ organised.

5 Sorry, I think I _____ understood you. Can you explain what you mean?

6 The architect has built a _____ rail to help passengers travel from one side of the city to the other.

7 His success was _____ shadowed by one small mistake.

8 Guess what! I've got tickets for the _____ finals of the tennis. Would you like to come with me?

9 This injection may cause a little _____ comfort.

10 Carl Jung _____ defined our understanding of psychology in the 20th century.

11 The greatest athletes always try to_____ perform their last record.

12 She's a really _____ rated singer and much better than everyone in the newspapers say.

13 Your answer to this question is _____ correct. Try again.

14 The latest government report proposed _____ lingual education in schools.

GRAMMAR: present simple and present continuous

2 Underline the correct verb forms in this article.

If you are the President of the USA, what [1] _do you do/ are you doing_ when you lose your job? The answer is easy. You [2] _start/are starting_ giving talks about being the President! That's what's happened to Bill Clinton. He [3] _makes/'s making_ between nine and ten million dollars a year by giving speeches all over the world, from Australia to Egypt. This [4] _compares/is comparing_ well with the $200,000 salary a year he received as President of the USA. With around 350 talks a year, his present schedule means that he [5] _probably gives/ is probably giving_ a talk somewhere in the world at the same time as you [6] _read/are reading_ this. Currently, he [7] _also tries/'s also trying_ to raise even more money for his charity which he [8] _runs/is running_ to combat HIV/Aids.

3 Complete this email to your friend called Jules. Use the words to write sentences in the present simple or the present continuous.

Hi Jules
how / you?
How are you?
I / work / in the office / the moment
(1) _____
but my boss always / lunch / 12
(2) _____
…so I / write / you while he's out.
(3) _____
you / have / good time / Barcelona at the moment?
(4) _____
what / you / think of your course?
(5) _____
how / weather?
(6) _____
it / rain / here!
(7) _____
Wish I was with you!
Love Rachel

READING

4 Read the article and write each verb in brackets in the present simple or present continuous form.

Do you worship celebrities?

Do you wake up every night thinking of your favourite singer? Or do you wonder what a TV presenter ¹ _has_ (have) for breakfast in the morning? If so, you may have a newly identified psychological condition: Celebrity Worship Syndrome (CWS). Following a recent study, psychologists at the University of Leicester now ² _____ (believe) that one in three of us are obsessed with celebrities and the number ³ _____ (go up).

One theory is that our modern lives ⁴ _____ (become) more and more dominated by TV and so modern celebrities often ⁵ _____ (take) the place of relatives, neighbours and close friends for many people.

The study of around 700 people aged 18 to 60 ⁶ _____ (show) that there are three types of Celebrity Worship Syndrome. The largest number of people – 22 percent of the study – only ⁷ _____ (have) a small problem and they are likely to be extroverts with a passion for talking about their chosen celebrity. Another 12 percent have an intense personal type of relationship with their idol, while the third group, with the most extreme CWS, ⁸ _____ (think) their celebrity knows them. These people are often introverts, anti-social and insensitive.

Fortunately, most people's interest in the rich and famous is perfectly normal and healthy. Dr John Maltby of Leicester University says, 'It is not necessarily a bad thing. Many people are interested in celebrities.' However, says Dr Maltby, 'We ⁹ _____ (begin) to define CWS for the first time and research is suggesting that, generally, people with CWS ¹⁰ _____ (replace) normal relationships with these fantasy relationships.'

5 What do these numbers and figures from the reading refer to? Match 1–5 to a–e.

1 one in three   _c)_

2 700   ____

3 60   ____

4 22 percent   ____

5 12 percent   ____

a) the maximum age of people in the study

b) people with the first type of CWS

c) the ratio of people with CWS

d) people with the second type of CWS

e) the number of people in the study

LISTENING

6 [1.4] Listen to someone being interviewed as part of the study on CWS. Complete the researcher's questions.

1 _____ ?

Sport, especially football.

2 _____ ?

Ronaldhino.

3 _____ ?

Of course.

4 _____ ?

Fairly.

5 _____ ?

I've no idea.

6 _____ ?

Quite often.

7 _____ ?

Johnny Depp (met him at a first night première).

8 _____ ?

Not often.

KEY LANGUAGE: giving opinions, agreeing and disagreeing

1 Put each phrase a–h in the correct place to complete the conversation.

a) don't know

b) come on

c) great idea

d) don't agree

e) how about

f) I suggest

g) I think

h) it's true

A: ¹ __g__ Roger is the best person for the team. After all, he scored very well on the psychometric test.

B: Well, ²_____ that he scored well, but do you really want another ambitious, self-confident extrovert on the team?

A: ³_____ ! You make him sound awful. He's a nice person.

B Well, I ⁴_____ . He seems a bit over-confident. But the main issue is that we already have two big characters on the team. ⁵_____ we take on someone who is quieter and gets on with the hard work. Otherwise, we'll have too many egos.

A: OK. I ⁶_____ with you about Roger but let's look at the alternatives.

B: ⁷_____ Petra? She's nice and she seems like the sort of person who gets on with everyone.

A: That's a ⁸_____ ! I'd forgotten about her. Maybe I'll be able to put Roger on another project.

2 Rewrite the first sentence with the same meaning using the words given.

1 We could employ Magda, couldn't we?

Why don't we _____ ?

2 We should call him and see if he wants the job.

I suggest _____ .

3 What if we give them all a team task?

How about _____ ?

4 I think we ought to check their references before we decide?

What about _____ ?

5 How do you feel about Petra?

_____ think about Petra?

6 I think Michael's right.

I agree _____ .

PRONUNCIATION: sentence stress

3a `1.5` Listen to five mini-dialogues. Which word in each response is stressed? Tick the version with the correct word in bold, a, b or c.

1 I don't believe he's sixty!

a) **Well**, it's true.

b) Well, **it's** true.

c) Well, it's **true.** ✓

2 Let's go out tonight.

a) **That's** a great idea.

b) That's a **great** idea.

c) That's a great **idea.**

3 In my opinion, she's the best person for the job.

a) **I** don't agree.

b) I **don't** agree.

c) I don't **agree.**

4 I don't think we'll find the right person in the company.

a) I **suggest** we try.

b) I suggest **we** try.

c) I suggest we **try.**

5 Who can we ask to do this?

a) **How** about Ben?

b) How **about** Ben?

c) How about **Ben?**

6 She drives me mad!

a) **Come** on. She's OK.

b) Come **on.** She's OK.

c) Come on. She's **OK.**

7 How do you feel about it?

a) **I** think it's fine.

b) I **think** it's fine.

c) I think it's **fine.**

3b `1.5` Listen again and practise saying the sentences.

STUDY SKILLS: taking notes while reading

TAKE NOTES BETTER

When you take notes, write down the key words such as names, numbers and key verbs or nouns.

1 Look back at the article about Bill Clinton on page 7 and complete these notes.

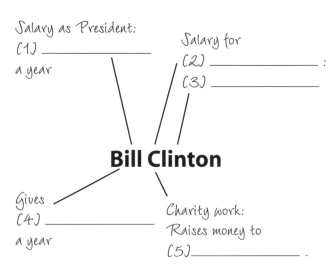

Salary as President:
(1) _____ a year

Salary for
(2) _____ :
(3) _____

Bill Clinton

Gives
(4) _____ a year

Charity work:
Raises money to
(5) _____ .

WRITING: comparative essay

2 Write the missing linking words in sentences 1–8. The first letter of each word is given.

1 It's still the case that more men than women become politicians. H*owever*, it is slowly changing with more and more women entering politics.

2 A_____ people should be fined for speeding in cars, I don't think the police should use cameras.

3 Using abbreviations helps with note-taking. For e_____ , you can use the symbol '>' instead of writing 'is greater than'.

4 D_____ the fact that everyone is talking about climate change and global warming, we don't seem to be doing much to solve the problem.

5 Many men become managers. This is b_____ they rarely take career breaks.

6 In c_____ to men, many women take career breaks to have children.

7 To s_____ up, six is probably the maximum number of people you want on most teams.

8 On b_____ , women are probably safer drivers than men.

3 A student is writing two paragraphs for an essay titled: 'Are women better at working in teams than men?' Write these missing sentences in the correct places in the paragraph.

a) women make decisions more slowly

b) they also enjoy being in groups

c) they like to lead groups

d) ~~women are better listeners~~

e) men are more likely to disagree and argue

f) women like to discuss ideas

g) men are usually in charge

Some people believe that women are better at working in teams than men. There are various reasons for this. Firstly, 1 _d) and 2 _____ . Secondly, 3 _____ with other people.

On the other hand, 4 _____ than men. In addition, 5 _____ of teams because 6 _____ . Despite this, 7 _____ with other members of the team.

2 Travel

2.1 TOURISM AND TRAVELLING

**VOCABULARY:
travel expressions**

1 Read the clues below and write the missing travel words in this crossword.

Across

1 The place you travel to.

4 The place where bags are checked for illegal items.

6 To go on a journey.

7 A kind of journey.

8 The industry which helps people to go on holiday.

10 You pay this to protect yourself on holiday.

Down

1 Papers with official information for travel (e.g. passport, tickets, visa).

2 To live in a place for a temporary period.

3 You have this to protect against a disease.

5 A special place to see (e.g. famous monument, building, palace).

9 To come together with new people on holiday.

2 Write one of these verbs in each sentence 1–10.

| get | respect | find out | see | broaden |
| become | explore | find | | |

1 I think it's good for young people to take a gap year and travel to _____ their horizons.

2 We're going to _____ some old temples in the mountains.

3 Lots of people travel to _____ themselves as much as to visit new places.

4 I like holidays where you just _____ away from it all on a beach doing nothing.

5 My daughter has _____ more independent since her trip to Thailand.

6 So what sights did you _____ while you were there?

7 It's important to _____ the local culture and act in the correct way.

8 Did you _____ what time the train leaves for Rome?

EXTRA VOCABULARY: word pairs

3 Make pairs of words for talking about holidays by matching a word in A to a word in B. Then complete the sentences 1–5 with each pair.

A	B
insurance	agent
dress	tour
holiday	codes
package	policy
travel	resort

1 Remember to take out an *insurance policy* before you go on holiday in case of an emergency.

2 We used to book with a _____ but now we book online.

3 They've built a new _____ on the coast. It's so ugly!

4 _____ in some countries can be quite formal.

5 We booked a _____ which included the bus and all our meals.

READING

1 Read this biography about the travel writer, Bruce Chatwin. Complete the timeline of his life with events 1–9. See the example.

Bruce Chatwin was born on 13 May 1940 but his interest in writing grew later on in his life. He started his career at the auction house Sotherby's, where he soon became the expert on Impressionist art. But in 1964 he went on a journey to Ethiopia and his interest in archaeology began. He studied archaeology for a year at university but found academic study boring and left.

In 1972 *The Sunday Times Magazine* employed him to write about art and architecture. The job improved his writing skills and also gave him the chance to travel. In 1977 he flew to Patagonia. He spent six months there and wrote the highly successful book *In Patagonia*.

Chatwin carried on writing both fiction and travel books for the rest of his life, including the famous *Songlines* about the Aborigines in Australia. In his career, Chatwin received praise for his story-telling abilities and criticism from others for not telling the truth in his books. In the late 1980s Chatwin developed AIDS and died in 1989.

1 Went to Ethiopia	6 Wrote his first book
2 Died	7 University for a year
3 Became a journalist	8 Wrote *Songlines*
4 ~~Chatwin born~~	9 Travelled to Patagonia
5 Worked at Sotherby's	

4

|___|__|____|___|___|_|___|____|

1940   1964   1972 1977   1989

VOCABULARY: phrasal verbs (1)

2 Match the verb to the particle and complete the sentences.

set	get	stop	out	on	off
get	look	carry	around	back	to

1 Marco Polo *set out* in 1271 with his father to China.

2 Let's _____ _____ in Venice for a few days before continuing to Greece.

3 What time do we _____ _____ our destination?

4 I'll call you when I _____ _____ from my trip to Mexico.

5 Do you have any time to _____ _____ our city while you're here?

6 The bus stops here so we'll have to _____ _____ by foot.

EXTRA VOCABULARY: travel phrasal verbs

3 In each sentence, replace the words in bold with a phrasal verb. Write the verb next to the sentence.

~~check in~~	stop over	pull over
get in	take off	check out

1 You need to **go to the airline desk** two hours before the plane leaves. *check in*

2 What time do you have to **go to the hotel reception and pay**? _____

3 What time does the plane **arrive**? _____

4 When does the plane **leave**? _____

5 We'll probably **stay** in Singapore for a day in between our two flights. _____

6 I'm lost. **Park the car at the side of the road** and we can look at the map. _____

GRAMMAR: past simple

4 Read this page from an explorer's diary. Write each verb in brackets in the past simple.

1

We ¹_____ (start) our journey in October. Three of us ²_____ (leave) early in the morning and the rest of the group ³_____ (follow) us an hour later. The group ⁴_____ (walk) all day and in the evening we ⁵_____ (find) a small lake with fresh water. The desert ⁶_____ (be) cold but very beautiful. My colleagues ⁷_____ (photograph) the night sky until finally we ⁸_____ (go) to bed. In the morning the team ⁹_____ (continue) the journey but it ¹⁰_____ (become) harder and harder to walk in the heat...

5 Write these verbs in the quiz below in the past simple. Afterwards test your own knowledge and complete the quiz. See the answers on page 93.

| be   reach   lead   make   sail |

Test your knowledge of the Great Explorers!

1 Who _____ the South Pole first?

A Robert Scott

B Roald Amundsen

C Richard Branson

2 Who _____ the first expedition westwards from Europe to Asia via the Pacific?

A Ferdinand Magellan

B Marco Polo

C Vasco da Gama

3 Who _____ the second man on the moon?

A Yuri Gagarin

B Neil Armstrong

C Edwin Aldrin

4 Who _____ to America first?

A The Vikings

B Christopher Columbus

C James Cook

5 Which European first _____ contact with the continent of Australia?

A Thor Heyerdahl

B Captain James T Kirk

C Captain James Cook

PRONUNCIATION: -ed endings

6a How many syllables are each word, 1, 2 or 3? Write your answer next to the word.

1 invented *3 (in –vent – ed)*

2 danced _____

3 discussed _____

4 decided _____

5 travelled _____

6 arrived _____

7 introduced _____

8 landed _____

9 worked _____

10 lifted _____

6b `1.6` Listen to check your answers and practise saying the words.

DICTATION

7 `1.7` Listen and complete the next page in the explorer's diary.

We _____ the desert for another and _____ mountains.

During this time, _____ _____ feel sick. _____ _____ but the journey _____ .

Then, _____ ,

some people _____ and _____ to their tents.

_____ . Their

leader was an old man and _____

_____ . We _____ what the

medicine was but _____

_____ . The people

in the desert _____

_____ and _____

_____ .

GRAMMAR: present perfect and past simple

1 Match the two halves of the sentences.

1 Ralph hasn't been to Europe _____

2 He's _____

3 Has he been _____

4 He's never _____

5 Ralph went there _____

6 He's already been to three capital cities this _____

7 Has Ralph _____

a) before?

b) week.

c) been before.

d) yet.

e) ever been to Europe?

f) already been there.

g) when he was a boy.

TRANSLATION

2 Translate the sentences 1–7 in Exercise 1 into your language.

1 _____

_____

2 _____

_____

3 _____

_____

4 _____

_____

5 _____

_____

6 _____

_____

7 _____

_____

3 Read this email and underline the correct form, present perfect or past simple.

Dear Petra

How [1] *have you been/were you*? I think the last time we [2] *'ve spoken/spoke* was over two months ago. Anyway I [3] *'ve just returned/just returned* from a week walking in Morocco. We [4] *have flown/flew* to Marrakesh and then [5] *have walked/walked* for three days in the Atlas mountains. I [6] *'ve never done/never did* anything in my life so tiring but so amazing before! The tour leader [7] *has taken/took* us to parts of the mountains where tourists don't normally go and the local people [8] *have invited/invited* us in to their homes. At the end, the group [9] *have spent/spent* a night in Fez with its ancient markets. I [10] *haven't spent/didn't spend* too much money there but I [11] *have bought/bought* a couple of really beautiful ornaments. Anyway, I [12] *'ve already booked/already booked* another holiday there in the autumn. Would you like to come?

PRONUNCIATION: contracted form ('s / 've)

4 [1.8] Listen to six sentences. Tick the sentence you hear.

1 I travelled all night.

I've travelled all night.

2 He climbed this mountain.

He's climbed this mountain.

3 They worked here for years.

They've worked here for years.

4 She told him the news.

She's told him the news.

5 We talked to them.

We've talked to them.

6 It hit the building.

It's hit the building.

READING

5 Read about Martin Strel and write the verbs in the past simple or the present perfect.

Sharks, stingrays and crocodiles: swimming the Amazon at 52

There ¹ _____ (be) a time when explorers ² _____ (tell) us about their amazing adventures in books. But nowadays, no 'true' adventurer or explorer travels without a documentary film crew. And so Martin Strel, a 52-year-old Slovakian, ³ _____ (take) camera men to the Amazon with him. Last week they ⁴ _____ (begin) filming Strel's attempt to swim the length of the river. On the first afternoon, they ⁵ _____ (film) him successfully swim through parts of the river in Peru. In the past, these sections of the river ⁶ _____ (stop) passenger ships. But Strel ⁷ _____ (survive) many previous dangers. As a young man, he ⁸ _____ (swim) the English channel and since then he ⁹_____ (also/swim) the Danube, Mississippi and Yangtze rivers. The Amazon, however, ¹⁰ _____ (be) a greater challenge for Strel with its crocodiles, stingrays and sharks. In case of emergencies, his back-up team ¹¹ _____ (pack) animal food to throw to any interested meat-eaters and his medical team ¹² _____ (take) a supply of blood from Mr Strel before the journey began – just in case the worst happens!

LISTENING

6 Write questions about Martin Strel's adventure in the past simple or present perfect.

1 Q: In the past, how_____ ?

 A: In books.

2 Q: Who _____ ?

 A: A film crew, a back-up team and a medical team

3 Q: What _____ ?

 A: Strel's attempt to swim the Amazon.

4 Q: What _____ ?

 A: Passenger ships.

5 Q: Why _____ ?

 A: For emergencies.

7 [1.9] Listen to part of a lecture about the travel writer Robert Byron. Decide if the statements 1–7 are true or false.

1 Byron was from France. ____

2 No one had written books about travel before *The Road to Oxiana*. ____

3 Byron also wrote about architecture. ____

4 *The Road to Oxiana* was his first book. ____

5 It was about his journey to Afghanistan. ____

6 It has been translated. ____

7 Byron died on one of his journeys. ____

8 Answer these questions about Byron.

1 Who has said it is the first example of great travel writing?

 _____

2 When was Byron born?

 _____

3 When did he publish his first book?

 _____

4 How long after *First Russia, Then Tibet* did he write *The Road to Oxiana*?

 _____

5 Which of his books is known worldwide?

 _____

KEY LANGUAGE: discussing advantages and disadvantages

1 **1.10** Listen to the conversation and tick the correct answers.

1 What is one advantage of eco-tourism?

  a) It's cheap.

  b) It's in interesting places.

  c) It's in different parts of the world.

2 What is one disadvantage of eco-tourism?

  a) It has lots of people.

  b) It causes more problems.

  c) It's in different parts of the world.

3 Why can't they go?

  a) They can't afford it.

  b) They can't agree.

  c) They both disagree with eco-tourism.

4 What kind of holiday don't they want?

  a) A package holiday.

  b) A sightseeing holiday.

  c) A beach holiday.

5 What can you find on an archaeological dig?

  a) Old buildings.

  b) The desert.

  c) The beach.

2 Match a beginning 1–7 with an ending a–g, to make the correct expressions.

1 I suggest	a) a good idea to …
2 How	b) we …
3 On the one hand	c) for and against.
4 I think we	d) should …
5 There are arguments	e) but on the other hand …
6 It'd be	f) about …
7 Another disadvantage	g) is that …

3 Use parts of the expressions in Exercise 2 to complete this discussion.

A: Have you thought any more about where to go on holiday?

B: Yes, I was reading about something called eco-tourism. I think ¹ _____ do something like that. What do you think?

A: Well, I've read about that too, and there are ² _____ .

B: What do you mean?

A: Well. on the ³ _____ you fly to interesting places and help with projects, but on the ⁴ _____ having lots of people travelling to parts of the world with ecological problems is probably causing more problems. Another ⁵ _____ is that we don't have enough money to do that! It's quite expensive.

B: So, where should we go?

A: Well, I agree that it'd be ⁶ _____ do something different rather than just sitting on a beach. ⁷ _____ about going on an archaeological dig?

B: What's that exactly?

A: Well you travel to an ancient place and help dig for old buildings and objects. A friend of mine is working on one in the Sahara desert. I ⁸ _____ we should join.

4 **1.10** Listen and check your answers. Practise saying the conversation.

LISTEN BETTER

When you take notes, listen for the key words such as nouns, verbs and adjectives. These are the words that are normally **stressed** in sentences.

1 ▦ 1.11 **Listen to these sentences and underline the words or parts of words (syllables) which are stressed.**

1 Amelia Earhart was born in Kansas.

2 She attended Columbia University in nineteen nineteen.

3 She went to her first air show in nineteen twenty.

4 Her first record was to fly at fourteen thousand feet.

5 Most people remember her as the first woman to fly solo non-stop across the Atlantic.

6 She took off from New Brunswick.

7 She published two books about her experiences.

2 ▦ 1.9 **Listen to the lecture about Robert Byron again. This time, complete the notes below about him.**

ROBERT BYRON:

British [1] _____

Born in [2] _____

[3] _____ at Oxford

Wrote about [4] _____ and

[5] _____

[6] _____ on _____ in the Second World War

Titles of famous books:

First [7] _____ *, Then*

[8] _____ (1933)

The [9] _____ *to Oxiana* (1937)

WRITING: a biographical profile

3 **Underline the correct time linker in each sentence.**

1 *After/During* qualifying as a teacher, I moved to France.

2 *Before/After* they met in Australia, both of them had worked in offices.

3 *During/While* that time, they got married.

4 I first met him *during/when* we were both at university.

5 I gave up my job *after/when* only a year.

6 She moved to New York *before/while* her friend was there. They shared a flat.

7 She took a gap year *while/when* she left university.

8 He wrote the book *while/during* he was living in Tibet.

9 I need to call them *after/before* they go abroad. Do you have their home number?

10 I worked as a secretary and *during/when* that time I saved all my money to go around the world.

4 **Number these sentences from a short biography in the correct order (1 to 5).**

____ But before I had finished my first year, I decided to leave and travel.

____ While we were living there, I started a degree in business at the university.

____ In 2003, during a trek in the Himalayas, I met my wife, Angela.

____ After we had finished our journey round the world together, we started an online tourist business, specialising in tourism to exotic places.

____ In 1995 my family moved to Brussels when my father took a job there.

3 Work

3.1 JOBS

VOCABULARY: work adjectives

1 Each speaker is describing a job. Match the adjective to the description. There is one extra adjective.

| glamorous | exciting | ~~rewarding~~ |
| challenging | flexible | stressful | repetitive |

1
> I get a lot of satisfaction from helping people in my work and the pay is good too! *rewarding*

2
> Every day presents a new problem which I like to solve.
> _____

3
> When I say I'm an actor everyone thinks I must have an amazing lifestyle of champagne, meeting celebrities and appearing in magazines. And they're right. I love it!
> _____

4
> My wife's job involves long hours and people constantly complaining.
> _____

5
> Every day is the same. I start at 9. I finish at 5. I meet the same people. I answer the same phone calls. It's so boring.
> _____

6
> My friend works for a company where you choose what hours you work and when you take a holiday. _____

PRONUNCIATION

2 Match the words in Exercise 1 to the stress patterns.

O o   *stressful*

O o o   _____ , _____ , _____

o O o   _____ , _____

o O o o _____

3 ⬛1.12 Listen to the words in Exercise 2 and check your answers. Practise saying the words.

EXTRA VOCABULARY: prepositions

4 Underline the correct preposition in these adverts.

> We are looking ¹ *on/for/to* an experienced individual who is able to work alone. You will be responsible ² *for/in/of* the running of our new Madrid office whilst reporting ³ *for/to/on* a manager in south-east of England.

> Fluency ⁴ *in /for/on* Spanish is essential and a good knowledge ⁵ *of/in/with* Portuguese is preferred for dealing with our Latin American clients, as well as the ability to communicate with people from all cultural backgrounds.
>
> Salary will depend ⁶ *on/of/in* experience.

> The post comes with excellent long-term prospects ⁷ *of/to/for* a candidate with a proven track record, preferably with experience ⁸ *in/for/on* planning budgets.

TRANSLATION

5 Do these jobs exist in your country? Can you translate them into your language?

1 Personal assistant _____

2 Sales manager _____

3 Finance director _____

4 Chief administrator _____

5 Marketing executive _____

6 Chief executive officer _____

What is your job title (or what job would you like to do in the future)? Can you translate it into English?

READING AND VOCABULARY

READ BETTER

With this type of reading exercise, remember to:
- read the whole text first.
- think about the words before AND after the gap.
- look for collocations.

1 Read this text about 'Extreme Commuters'. Look at 1–10 and complete each gap in the text with the correct missing word, a, b or c.

'EXTREME COMMUTERS'

AND WHY DO WE NEED THREE CUPHOLDERS?

In recent years, advances in technology have given us greater ¹ _____ opportunities with new ways of working such as telecommuting and ² _____ . But new figures from the US Census Bureau suggest the ³ _____ for long commutes to work may not have ended. In fact, 'extreme commuting' is increasing.

'Extreme commuters' can ⁴ _____ 90 minutes travelling to work one way. It seems that more ⁵ _____ than ever are still prepared to take time-⁶ _____ journeys in return for a big house in the country. This search for the perfect work-life ⁷ _____ means that nearly 10 million people now drive more than an hour to work, That's up by 50 percent ⁸ _____ 1990.

One effect of this is that one in every four restaurant meals are now eaten in the car and, to help our time ⁹ _____ , carmakers are adding extra cupholders, refrigeration boxes and even passenger seats which turn into dining tables. So the next time your colleague ¹⁰ _____ a lunch break, don't be surprised if it's in the car!

1 a) time-saving   b) job   c) workstation

2 a) housework   b) homework   c) homeworking

3 a) trend   b) rise   c) drive

4 a) use   b) spend   c) save

5 a) employment   b) unemployed   c) employees

6 a) consuming   b) saving   c) management

7 a) home   b) balance   c) style

8 a) since   b) in   c) by

9 a) for   b) clock   c) management

10 a) makes   b) takes   c) does

2 Read the article again and choose the correct answer.

1 What are people spending more time doing?

a) Working.

b) Travelling to work.

c) Drinking coffee.

2 What would many extreme commuters prefer to do?

a) Work longer to buy a big house.

b) Travel longer to live in a big house.

c) Travel less to live in a small house.

3 What has gone up by 50 percent since 1990?

a) The number of people with cupholders.

b) The number of people with a car.

c) The number of people driving for over two hours per day to and from work.

4 What do one in four of us now do?

a) Eat in cars.

b) Eat in restaurants.

c) Eat out at lunchtime.

3 Look again at the words in 1–10, in Exercise 1. Choose six of the words you didn't use in your answers and write six sentences. For example:

A workstation is the place where you work in the office with your computer.

1 _____

2 _____

3 _____

4 _____

5 _____

6 _____

LISTENING

LISTENING

4 [1.13] **Listen to the conversation between Sandy and Frieda and complete sentences 1–5.**

1 When Sandy arrives, Frieda

 a) finishes the book.

 b) stops reading.

 c) continues reading.

2 The detective in her book started chasing the 'bad guy'

 a) last month.

 b) for a month.

 c) months ago.

3 Sandy has

 a) passed her exams.

 b) looked for a job.

 c) to take her exams.

4 Frieda's company has promised her a promotion

 a) once.

 b) last month.

 c) many times.

5 Sandy thinks Frieda should

 a) leave the company.

 b) ask for a promotion.

 c) work longer.

GRAMMAR: present perfect continuous

5a **Write the verbs in this conversation in the present perfect continuous.**

F: Hi Sandy.

S: Hi Frieda. Sorry I'm late. How long [1] _have_ you _been waiting_ (wait)?

F: Not long. It's OK. I [2] _____ (read) my book. It's about a detective. He [3] _____ (chase) this bad guy for months. I've just got to the final chapter. Anyway, what [4] _____ you _____ (do) today?

S: I was with a friend. We [5] _____ (study) for our exams.

F: What do you think you'll do after university?

S: I haven't spent any time on that yet. I just want to pass these exams first. What about you? How's the job?

F: Well, my company [6] _____ (promise) me a promotion for months but nothing's happened.

S: Well, you [7] _____ (work) there a long time. Maybe it's time to move on…

5b [1.13] **Listen again and check your answers.**

6 **Complete each sentence with since or for.**

1 I've been working here _____ 2003.

2 He's been in charge _____ Kasia left.

3 I've been waiting for a reply _____ over a fortnight.

4 Maria has been out of work _____ June.

5 We've only been here _____ a few minutes.

6 Lisa hasn't seen her family _____ she was a child.

7 There have been a lot of changes _____ they arrived.

8 My friend and I have been trying to solve this problem _____ a week now.

DICTATION

7 [1.14] **Listen to part of a job interview and write in the missing words. I: Interviewer, C: Candidate**

I: So in your current job I see that _____ _____ from home. How long _____ _____ that?

C: Well, I _____ my employer for about three and a half years but after a couple of years I was able to _____ _____ .

I: So, how _____ ? I mean, _____ it?

C: Actually, it's one of the reasons I'd like to change jobs. I love my work but I miss _____ _____ . That's one of the things which _____ to this post.

I: So if we offered you _____ _____ ?

C: Well, obviously if the job required it, then that would be fine. But I _____ _____ people. I think that's one of my strengths – my ability to communicate.

READING

1 Read the information leaflet about interviews. Choose the correct heading, a–f, for each paragraph.

a) Show you are interested

b) The handshake

c) Make every second count

d) First impressions

e) The eyes and the mouth

f) Use your body

1 _____

From the moment an interviewer meets you, he or she forms an idea about what sort of person you are, and what kind of employee you would make.
So how can you appear more confident, even if you are feeling nervous?

2 _____

When we are nervous, we tend to walk more slowly and look indecisive. Alan Powers, an expert in body language, says that when an interviewee walks into the interview room, he or she should pause at the door and then walk confidently.

3 _____

When you shake hands, hold it with a strong grip but also be friendly. A weak grip means a weak character whereas if you are too strong, you won't impress the interviewer either.

4 _____

It's important to look interested and attentive but don't stare at your potential boss. And SMILE from time to time! It also helps you to relax.

5 _____

Sit up and be interested. Lean forward and avoid crossing your arms or legs. According to Powers, it can also be helpful to 'copy' the interviewer's movements. Copying, or what Powers calls 'mirroring', is a way for us to tell others that we think in the same way.

6 _____

'You never get a second chance', says image consultant Jane Chapman: 'Interviews only give you a short time to show who you are. By using body language and dress, you can start as soon as you get through the door.'

2 Read the leaflet again and decide if these statements are true or false.

1 Interviewers usually don't form an opinion about you until you start answering their questions. ____

2 The speed at which you walk will tell the interviewer how you feel. ____

3 When you shake someone's hand, a really strong grip is always best. ____

4 Don't stop smiling and when you talk, make sure what you say is interesting. ____

5 Try to copy what the interviewer says and always agree with him or her. ____

6 Think about how you can use every moment of the interview to make sure you get that job. ____

EXTRA VOCABULARY: noun combinations

3 Match a word from each column to make noun combinations about work and interviews.

shock	details
contact	tactics
survey	agency
past	experience
killer	results
customer	question
recruitment	appearance
smart	services

4 Complete sentences 1–8 with noun combinations from Exercise 3.

1 Can you tell me if these _contact_ _details_ are correct? For example, is your telephone number still 0207 859 6877?

2 _____ _____ show that 68 percent of employers rate real life experience more highly than qualifications.

3 The interview was awful. She asked me a _____ _____ about which famous celebrity I would invite to dinner.

4 At an interview, I like to ask simple questions and then I use _____ _____ to throw the candidate off guard.

5 Tell me a little about your _____ _____ with your previous employer. Did you enjoy working there?

6 Hello. _____ _____. How can I help you today?

7 I've registered with a _____ _____ . I hope they find me some work soon.

8 I think a _____ _____ can make all the difference at an interview. After all, 70 percent of what we think about a person is based on how they look.

GRAMMAR: present perfect simple and continuous

5 **Underline the correct form of the verb.**

1 I *'ve done/'ve been doing* my essay and handed it in.

2 I *'ve done/'ve been doing* my essay and I still need to write the conclusion.

3 They*'ve replied/'ve been replying* to all one hundred people so that's an end to it.

4 He*'s talked/'s been talking* on the phone since 10 o'clock so I haven't been able to see him yet.

5 How much money *have you spent/have you been spending* since last week?

6 How long *have you waited/have you been waiting* for their decision? Why don't you give them a call and ask for their answer?

7 We've always *used/been using* this type of computer.

8 No-one has ever *complained/been complaining* before.

9 The photocopier*'s broken/'s been breaking* down again. That's the fifth time this month.

10 How many people *have applied/have been applying* so far?

6 **Underline the correct phrase.**

1 I've been writing and sending letters *already/all day*.

2 We've employed twenty new workers *in the last three weeks/for months*.

3 You've answered five questions *in the last hour/for an hour*.

4 I've been asking them about this *for days/three times*.

5 They asked me really difficult questions *at the interview/over the interview*.

6 She's had lots of interviews over the *years/hour*.

7 They've interviewed 10 people *in three hours/all day long*.

8 He's been waiting since *over two hours/8 o'clock this morning*.

PRONUNCIATION

7a `1.15` **Listen to seven sentences. Circle the number of words you hear in each sentence. Contracted forms count as two words, for example, *they've*.**

Sentence 1:	5	6	7	8
Sentence 2:	3	4	5	6
Sentence 3:	6	7	8	9
Sentence 4:	3	4	5	6
Sentence 5:	6	7	8	9
Sentence 6:	5	6	7	8
Sentence 7:	6	7	8	9

7b `1.15` **Listen again and practise saying the sentences.**

8 **Look at these mini-dialogues. Write full questions using the present perfect simple or continuous form.**

1 Q: How long / you / write / that report?

   _____?

   A: About 6 hours.

2 Q: How many reports / you / write?

   _____?

   A: Six in total.

3 Q: Have / you / wait / a long time?

   _____?

   A: Yes, about an hour.

4 Q: Where / he / live?

   _____?

   A: In five different countries.

5 Q: Where / they / live?

   _____?

   A: In France since last year.

6 Q: Who / she / interview / all morning?

   _____?

   A: Candidates for the post of receptionist.

7 Q: How many / they / interview / this morning?

   _____?

   A: Two people. One of them was from Vietnam.

1 Match a verb to a noun to make verb + noun combinations about work.

VERBS	NOUNS
recruit	a plan
deal with	new markets
research	team
set	customers
serve	more staff
put together	costs
reduce	objectives
lead a	complaints

KEY LANGUAGE:
asking questions, giving answers

2 Match the correct ending a–g for the beginning of the framing questions 1–7.

1 Now, here's a question we like to ask everyone, ___

2 Let me follow that up ___

3 OK. Now moving on, can you tell me ___

4 I'm interested in ___

5 I was wondering what ___

6 Just one more thing I'd like to ask ___

7 A question now ___

a) knowing more about your studies.

b) where do you think you'll be in five years' time?

c) about your free time.

d) you think you can add to our company?

e) about is how long you intend to stay here?

f) about your previous job.

g) with another question.

3 Write one of these words in each response, 1–7.

ask	glad	moment	honest	question
detail	expert			

1 I'm _____ you asked me that.

2 That's a very interesting _____ .

3 Without going into too much _____ , my boss and I didn't agree.

4 Let me just think about that for a _____ .

5 I thought you might _____ me about that.

6 Well, I'm not an _____ , but I think the increase will continue.

7 To be _____ , I'm not sure.

LISTENING

4 Before you listen, can you guess the missing words in these interview questions? The first letter is given.

1 What kind of p*erson* are you?

2 What would you say is your biggest w_____ ?

3 What i_____ do you have outside work?

4 If you were an a_____ what would it be?

5 What do you think you can b_____ to this post?

6 How much of a t_____ player are you?

7 How do you think your c_____ would describe you?

8 Can you tell me about your q_____ ?

5 Now match questions 1–8 in Exercise 4, to answers (a–h)

a) Probably, that I tend to take my work home, though some people call that a strength I suppose. _____

b) Well, in my last job I learnt to use the latest technology. _____

c) That's a difficult one... a leopard, perhaps.

_____

d) Well, I have a degree in business studies and an MBA. _____

e) I think the people I work closely with would say I was supportive. _____

f) I think I'm quite outgoing. _____

g) I like cycling and visiting museums. _____

h) Well, I have plenty of experience of working with groups of people. _____

6 `1.16` Now listen and check your answers to Exercises 4 and 5. Practise saying the questions and answers.

7 Imagine you are at the job interview. Write your own answers for the questions.

STUDY AND WRITING SKILLS

STUDY SKILLS: organising ideas

1 Read sentences a–h below. They are from two different paragraphs: the first is about preparing for a job interview, the second is about what to wear. Put the two paragraphs in order and write your answers here:

Paragraph 1:　1 _e)_　2 ___　3 ___　4 ___

Paragraph 2:　5 _f)_　6 ___　7 ___　8 ___

a) This means that employees may be expected to wear ties.

b) For example, 'What are your greatest achievements?' and 'What is the company vision or philosophy?'.

c) On the other hand, some modern employers allow jeans and T-shirts.

d) As a general rule, it's better to be slightly over-dressed than make the mistake of appearing too casual.

e) There are two main points to consider when preparing for a job interview.

f) One important factor when deciding what to wear to an interview is to know what the dress code is at the company.

g) First of all, find out as much as you can about the company.

h) Second, try to predict the type of questions you might be asked and also prepare questions to ask.

WRITING: covering letter

2 Read the covering letter. Write the missing word in each line.

(0)　　Dear
⌃ Sir or Madam

(1) I writing to apply for the post of trainee journalist,

(2) you advertised in this morning's newspaper.

(3) I have always been interested current affairs and

(4) local politics and I like the opportunity to report on them.

(5) I am outgoing, confident person with good

(6) communication skills. In spare time I have also run

(7) the student newsletter my university.

(8) I am available at time convenient to you for an

(9) interview, where I look forward discussing my application.

3 A job applicant has seen this advert in a student magazine.

WANTED Summer school activities leader wanted to work with children (aged 11–15).

You will need to organise games such as football and netball and take the children on trips and visits.

Please send your CV with a covering letter to …

He has also made these notes to help him write the letter.

post – summer school activities leader
advertisement in student magazine
interests — rock climbing — team sports
outgoing — leadership skills - good with teenagers
interview – available any time

Now complete his covering letter using the information in the notes.

Dear Sir/Madam

I am writing to apply for _____
_____
_____
as advertised in _____ .

_____ .
I have been interested in outdoor activities for many years and in my spare time I _____
_____ .
_____ .
I am an _____
_____
_____ .
I am available _____ .
I look _____
you to discuss my application.

Yours faithfully,

4 Language

4.1 LEARNING LANGUAGES

VOCABULARY: language learning

1 Some students are talking about learning languages. Match one of these terms to each sentence.

grammar foreign languages bilingual
native speakers accent dialect slang

1 'I want to learn street English, for example, the informal words that people use with their friends.'

_____

2 'I'm OK with the grammar, but when I listen I find it really hard to understand the pronunciation of some native speakers.'

_____

3 'I like to try and talk to people who were born in a country where English is the first language.'

_____

4 'I love to find out the way language works and all the rules.'

_____

5 'They are really hard to learn. Why can't everyone just speak the same language as me!'

_____

6 'People with parents from different countries are really lucky because they can learn two languages from birth.'

_____

7 'It isn't just the fact that their accent is different, but their English even uses different words and incorrect grammar!'

_____

VOCABULARY: phrasal verbs (2)

2 Write the correct verb in each space. Change the verb form if necessary.

take pick catch fall keep let get

1 My poor English often _____ me down.

2 I'm quick to _____ on and learn new words.

3 She's currently _____ behind the rest of the class.

4 My friend _____ up languages really easily.

5 I'm not fluent but I can _____ by in French when I'm travelling.

6 I suggest you _____ up a new language in your free time.

7 Sorry, but I can't _____ up with you. Please speak more slowly.

PRONUNCIATION: linking

3a `1.17` When we speak in English, we often link a word ending with a consonant sound to the next word beginning with a vowel sound. Listen to these examples.

catch‿up / I need to catch‿up with my work.

picks‿up / She picks‿up languages quickly.

3b `1.18` Now listen to these sentences. Draw the links between words.

1 I can't keep up with the class.

2 Take up a hobby.

3 He catches on well.

4 She has a foreign accent.

5 I'm learning to drive a car.

6 Can I learn it easily?

3c `1.18` Listen again and practise saying the sentences.

GRAMMAR: future forms

1 There is one incorrect word in each sentence. Correct or delete it.

going
1 They're ~~go~~ to do media studies at university when they finish school.

2 I'm call you back in an hour.

3 People won't stopping travelling by plane in the future.

4 I'll probably to see you this evening.

5 We're going meeting at three this afternoon.

6 She'll going to join us at the Red Café.

7 When will you returning from Beijing?

8 Sorry, I'm not going to working here tomorrow so I can't help you.

2 Find one example of the following in sentences 1–8:

1 a prediction about the future: ___

2 a decision made at the time of speaking: ___

3 an intention for the future: ___

4 a fixed arrangement, plan or programme: ___

3 Write the verb in brackets in the best future form (***will, going to*** or ***the present continuous***).

1 I've made a decision and I _____ (apply) for a course in business.

2 They haven't made a decision yet but they think they _____ (probably/ leave) tomorrow morning.

3 We _____ (meet) them outside the concert hall at 7 p.m.

4 A: We've got a problem because we don't have enough people in the team.

   B: I've got an idea! I _____ (ask) my friend Mike. He plays soccer.

5 A: Do you want a game of tennis next week?

   B: Sorry, I _____ (go) to Jamaica on holiday on Saturday.

6 A: How do you intend to pay for it?

   B: I don't know.

   A: You could ask your father.

   B: Good idea. I _____ (do) that.

7 I don't think people _____ (use) SMS texting in the future.

8 We've booked the taxi. He _____ (pick) us up in the morning.

9 My parents _____ (sell) their house and buy a boat! I don't think we can change their minds.

10 A: When do you think we _____ (see) you again?

   B: I really don't know.

PRONUNCIATION: contracted forms

4a **1.19** Listen to eight sentences. Circle the number of words you hear in each sentence. Count a contracted form (*you'll, I'm, we're, he's*) as one word.

Sentence 1:	6	7	8	9
Sentence 2:	5	6	7	8
Sentence 3:	5	6	7	8
Sentence 4:	4	5	6	7
Sentence 5:	4	5	6	7
Sentence 6:	4	5	6	7
Sentence 7:	5	6	7	8
Sentence 8:	6	7	8	9

4b **1.19** Listen again and practise saying the sentences. Don't forget to use the contracted forms.

5 Underline the correct word, *allow, permit* or *let* in these sentences.

1 Will your parents *allow/let* you go out tonight?

2 The law doesn't *let/permit* anyone under age to drink in a bar.

3 My teacher won't *allow/let* me to go outside with my friends.

4 When I'm on a diet I *permit/allow* myself one ice cream once a week!

5 Please note that smoking is not *let/permitted* on this flight.

6 *Let/Permit* me try to do it.

EXTRA VOCABULARY: phrasal verbs for studying

6 In each sentence, replace the words in bold with one of these phrasal verbs. Write the verb with the pronoun in the correct position.

write up	note down	write out	read up on
read out	~~look up~~		

1 I don't know this word. I'll **find** it in my dictionary.
   look it up

2 I'm going to put sentences on the board and I'd like you to **copy** them in your notebooks.
   _____

3 For homework I'd like you to **complete** the notes from today's class **in full**. _____

4 Pablo, can you **say** your answers for this exercise so the class can hear? _____

5 I didn't understand everything in class today on the present perfect. I think I'll have to **find out about** it from grammar book at home tonight.
   _____

6 Listen to the tape and **write down** any important words you hear. _____

LISTENING

7 [1.20] A teacher is using a questionnaire to ask a student about how she learns English. Read the questionnaire and then listen. Tick the answers for the student.

HOW DO YOU LEARN NEW WORDS?

1 When you hear a word for the first time, do you
   a) look it up in a dictionary? ☐
   b) ask to hear it again? ☐
   c) repeat it a number of times to yourself? ☐

2 Do you write new words
   a) on cards? ☐
   b) in a notebook? ☐
   c) on the board? ☐

3 When you write a new word in your notebook, do you
   a) translate it? ☐
   b) write it in a useful sentence? ☐
   c) write a definition ? ☐

4 When you learn a word for the first time, do you also
   a) write its opposite (antonym)? ☐
   b) write a word with a similar meaning (synonym)? ☐
   c) try to make other words from it? ☐

5 Which technique do you use to revise new words?
   a) Write them on small pieces of paper and test yourself. ☐
   b) Choose seven new words and write a short story using them. ☐
   c) Try using them in sentences when talking to people in English. ☐

8 Now answer the questionnaire for yourself.

LEARN BETTER

When we learn new words, any of the ideas in the questionnaire could be helpful. Why not try some of the techniques you've never tried before?

DICTATION

9 [1.21] Listen to a news report on text messages. Write in the missing words.

New research figures show that _____ _____ _____ . This figure was up _____ on May and beat the previous monthly record of _____ _____ .

One representative for the research company said that _____ _____ .

She also predicted that _____ _____ . That _____ _____ up by nearly _____ _____ .

GRAMMAR: first conditional

1 Underline the correct verb form to make first conditional sentences.

1 If the government *spent/spends* more money on language teaching, foreign languages won't die out.

2 If we teach languages in schools, there *won't be/ isn't* time for subjects like maths or science.

3 Unless we *will work/work* harder, we won't finish on time.

4 If they revise more, they*'ll pass/passed* the exam.

5 When I *get/'ll get* to work, I'll check my diary.

6 If we leave now, we*'ll arrive/'re arriving* on time.

7 It *won't cost/costs* much if you book now.

8 You might learn more words, if you *study/will study* more.

2 Write the verb in brackets in the correct form to make first conditionals.

1 I _____ (see) you tonight, unless you change your mind.

2 We'll eat when you _____ (arrive).

3 You'll forget your French, if you _____ (not/use) it.

4 My daughter _____ (start) work as a doctor as soon as she's qualified.

5 No one will help you , if you _____ (not/ ask).

6 I _____ (not/come) if I'm not invited.

7 What will you say, if you _____ (see) him?

8 If the school doesn't offer French, where _____ (you/study) it?

LISTENING

3a `1.22` Two people from England are discussing languages in schools. Listen and answer these questions.

1 Who could spend more money to help language teaching?

2 What will children need to be in the future?

3 What else could children learn at school?

4 What will cost more money?

3b `1.22` Listen again and complete the notes in the table below

Arguments for	Arguments against
If you don't teach languages, they [1]_____ _____ _____ .	There are more important subjects like [4]_____ _____ .
In the future, children will need to be bilingual in order to [2]_____ _____ .	Language teaching in schools [5]_____ _____ _____ .
You also learn about [3]_____ _____ when you learn another language.	Children don't need other languages because [6]_____ _____ _____ .

PRONUNCIATION

4a Mark the intonation at the last word of each clause. Does it rise ⤴ or fall ⤵?

1 If we spend any more money, we won't have any left.

2 If we teach languages, they'll become bilingual.

3 Students won't have time for maths, if we teach English.

4 We don't need to learn a language, if everyone else speaks English.

4b `1.23` Now listen again and repeat.

READING

5 Read about American Sign Language. Decide if these statements are true or false according to the article.

1 People are 100% certain that languages such as French and German will disappear in the USA. ____

2 One American university has too many students for its courses in ASL. ____

3 ASL is easier to learn than a foreign language. ____

4 One ASL student also benefited by meeting other deaf people. ____

5 Douglas Baynton thinks people are critical of ASL because it's very strange and unusual. ____

6 Dr Lin believes you can say as much in ASL as you can in Chinese. ____

7 The student in the final paragraph believes people will understand the world as soon as they learn ASL. ____

6 Underline all the sentences using the first conditional in the article. How many sentences can you find?

ENROLMENT IN SIGN LANGUAGE CLASSES GROW

Some people believe that if more money and resources aren't given to traditional foreign language classrooms in the USA, languages such as French or German might die out. However, this doesn't mean that all language learning is in danger. More and more people are learning to speak with their hands.

One professor at an American university reports: 'If we offer American Sign Language (ASL), we'll have enough students for three courses. We cannot keep up with all the students who want to take the courses.'

One of the students also says, 'I just thought Sign Language was a beautiful language. I picked it up easily.'

Another student who has slowly lost her hearing since birth was also surprised by the course. 'Unless colleges offer these kinds of courses, deaf people will never really be part of society. The course also let me meet other people in the deaf community. It opened up a new world to me!'

However, some people have criticised the US schools offering American Sign Language. One reason is because some colleges won't accept it as a language if you can't speak it. Douglas Baynton, an ASL professor at University of Iowa, says: 'The idea that you can have a language on your hands is just very foreign.' ASL also uses space, gesture and body language.

But critics reply that ASL is not equal to languages like Chinese. Dr Lin, a professor of Chinese, comments that: 'If ASL is equal to traditional languages, it will have the same number of words and emotional range. In my opinion, it doesn't!'

But many ASL users say this is untrue. As one deaf student said: 'If you understand and use sign language, you'll understand the world the same as in any other language.'

KEY LANGUAGE: accepting and rejecting ideas; considering consequences

1 Put the words in order to make correct sentences.

1 I about that don't know.

I _____ .

2 If we will that it do some cause problems.

If _____ , _____ .

3 you right I 're think.

_____ .

4 I would think work that.

_____ .

5 I don't like I afraid 'm idea that.

_____ .

6 worth considering it definitely 's.

_____ .

7 I that not sure 'm about.

_____ .

8 what if happen that we do will.

_____ .

TRANSLATION

2 Translate the expressions in Exercise 1 into your language.

1 _____

_____

2 _____

_____

3 _____

_____

4 _____

_____

5 _____

6 _____

_____

7 _____

_____

8 _____

3 Use some of the words from sentences 1–8 in Exercise 1 to complete this discussion.

A: I wonder if we should offer English lessons to staff at lunchtime. What ¹ <u>will happen if we do that</u> ?

B: I'm afraid ² _____ . Staff will complain that we want them to work through their free time.

C: Yes, I ³ _____ . How about asking them about having a class after work?

A: I don't ⁴ _____ . The problem is that not everyone finishes work at the same time.

B: Yes, ⁵ _____ , it will also cause some problems with rooms. We have other courses in the training rooms.

A: What about making it voluntary? So people can choose.

B: Yes, I think ⁶ _____ .

C: It's definitely worth considering.

4a You are a teacher in a school. Write B's part in this discussion using some of the Key Language expressions and your own words.

A: I read a report that says if children learn a language from the age of four, it improves their intelligence. Do you think we should introduce Spanish classes for the younger pupils?

B: _____

_____ .

A: Yes, I think you're right. Let's do that. And we could also buy some computer programs for them to use during the lessons.

B: _____

_____ .

A: Well, I agree that it will be expensive initially, but once we've bought the software we can use it with the children year after year. And they like using the computers. I also thought we could start an after-school Spanish club. We'd have games and songs in Spanish for anyone interested. What do you think?

B: _____

_____ .

A: I'm glad you like the idea.

4b `1.24` Now listen to the dialogue and compare your version.

STUDY SKILLS: describing tables and charts

1 Underline the correct word to match each figure.

1 69% = just _over_/under two thirds

2 31% = just over/under a third

3 19% = slightly less than a half/fifth

4 52% = just over a half/quarter

5 75% = exactly/just less than three quarters

6 24.7% = approximately/slightly a quarter

7 52% = more/less than a half

8 40% = exactly two thirds/fifths

9 99.9% = almost/exactly everyone

10 91% = well/a little over three quarters

2 The chart shows feedback from 100 customers on a hotel's performance. Use fractions: _a quarter/a half/a third/a fifth_ to complete the sentences in the report below.

	Staff	Facilities	Room
Very satisfied	48	34	33
Satisfied	32	25	5
Quite satisfied	15	11	27
Not satisfied	5	11	33
No opinion	0	19	2

STAFF

1 Approximately _____ the customers were very satisfied with the staff's performance.

2 Nearly _____ were satisfied.

FACILITIES

3 Just over _____ were very satisfied with the facilities.

4 Exactly _____ were satisfied.

5 Almost _____ had no opinion.

ROOMS

6 Exactly _____ of customers said they were very satisfied and another _____ not satisfied.

7 Slightly over _____ were quite satisfied.

WRITING: a report

3 Look at these charts from a report. Complete the paragraph below.

Percentages of students learning foreign languages in school.

FIVE YEARS AGO

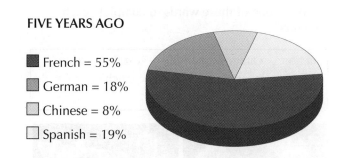

■ French = 55%
■ German = 18%
□ Chinese = 8%
□ Spanish = 19%

THIS YEAR

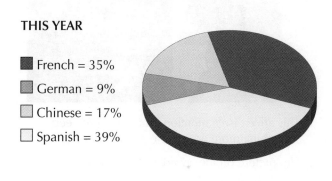

■ French = 35%
■ German = 9%
□ Chinese = 17%
□ Spanish = 39%

The two charts show _____
_____
_____
_____ .

The language with the biggest increase of _____
_____ has been _____ .

In addition, Chinese has also _____

by _____ .

However, the number of students learning French and
_____ has _____

by _____ and nine percent.

5 Advertising

5.1 WHAT MAKES A GOOD ADVERT?

32 UNIT 5 Advertising

VOCABULARY: adjectives, advertising

1 Write one of these words to complete each sentence.

action   catchy   grabbing   exotic   desire
attention   original   strong   catching
persuasive

 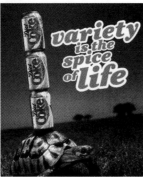

1 This advert isn't attention-*grabbing.* We need something more noticeable and memorable.

2 Her picture on the advert makes it very eye-_____ .

3 Coca-cola® has always been good at coming up with a _____ slogan.

4 Benetton adverts always use _____ images of people. Sometimes they can be quite shocking!

5 For any advert to work, it must get the customer's _____ .

6 An advert has to get your interest and create a _____ for the product.

7 The final part of the formula AIDA is that the buyer takes _____ .

8 I don't think many TV commercials are _____ . They've never convinced me to buy anything.

9 A good advert shows normal things in an _____ and completely new way.

10 When I first saw the advert I thought it was about holidays on an _____ beach but it turned out to be about chocolate!

TRANSLATION

2 Translate sentences 1–10 into your language.

1 _____
_____

2 _____
_____

3 _____
_____

4 _____
_____

5 _____
_____

6 _____
_____

7 _____
_____

8 _____
_____

9 _____
_____

10 _____
_____

PRONUNCIATION

3a 1.25 Listen and underline the stressed syllable in these words.

per<u>sua</u>sive   endorse

attention   slogan

promote   effective

sponsorship   logo

commercial   desire

exotic   misleading

3b 1.25 Now listen again and practise saying the words.

VOCABULARY: advertising methods

1 Some people are talking about different methods of advertising. Write the correct method after each sentence.

> word-of-mouth   TV commercials   leaflet
> endorsement   poster   radio spot
> side of bus

1 'I heard about it from my neighbour.'

_____

2 'There's one on the wall advertising the event. It's on Tuesday at 7.' _____

3 'I hate the way they come on and interrupt just when you're in the middle of a good movie.'

_____

4 'Someone just handed me this in the street. Normally I throw them away but this one is quite interesting actually.' _____

5 'Turn it up! I want to hear when the sale starts.'

_____

6 'I wouldn't buy anything that he was promoting!'

_____

7 'Follow it! I want to write down the telephone number at the bottom. Quick! It's turning left.'

_____

READING

2 Read the article about product placement in films and choose the best answer for each statement a, b or c.

1 When a new James Bond film is made

  a) only the film company benefits.

  b) not only film companies benefit.

  c) no one benefits.

2 The new Bond film

  a) contains lots of vodka.

  b) contains lots of product placement.

  c) contains lots of adverts.

3 All twenty companies have paid

  a) $70m dollars in total.

  b) $70m dollars per placement.

  c) too much money.

4 According to the article, some people don't like the new Bond movies because

  a) of the actor.

  b) there is too much advertising.

  c) of the poor advertising.

NEW BOND FILM IS A 'GIANT ADVERT'

The release of another James Bond film is always good business for firms outside the film industry as well as in. After over 40 years of Bond films, winning a place for products within a scene has become big business. So much so, that the latest Bond movie is, in some respects, one long advert for vodka, watches and cars.

Twenty companies will see their products on the big screen, having paid between them $70m (£44m) for the privilege. That is a record for product placement in a feature film. And the product placement is not even particularly subtle. After driving BMWs in his last three films, 007 is back behind the wheel of an Aston Martin. He has changed his vodka brand and ditched his Rolex watch. Some critics say some of the authentic Bond characteristics have been sacrificed because of advertising.

At a time when the advertising industry is in a downturn, it seems surprising that companies are falling over themselves to pay such huge sums. But brand consultant Steve King said that such a strategy makes sense. 'One of the unique things about cinema is its global appeal which means advertisers get the reach they cannot obtain elsewhere.'

The last three Bond films have made more than $1bn at the box office. Bond movies are especially popular with advertisers because of their appeal to the young and old. The 60–40 male-female ratio among Bond audiences is also appealing to many advertisers.

But where is product placement going? Experts say it may not be too long before interactive television and mobile technology link up. You will be able to buy the watch straight from James Bond's wrist. As advertisers continue to pay ever larger sums for the cachet of displaying their goods, the lines between advertising and entertainment are becoming increasingly blurred.

5 Advertisers prefer cinema because

  a) it attracts more people than TV.

  b) people will see the products all over the world.

  c) the films are better.

6 Bond films also reach an audience which is

  a) all generations and a high proportion of males.

  b) more women than men.

  c) a higher proportion of younger people.

7 The writer thinks it is becoming harder to know the difference between

  a) a TV show and a film.

  b) an advert and product placement.

  c) something you enjoy watching and an advert.

3 Find words in the reading text that mean the following:

1 attractive special quality _____

2 unique benefit _____

3 not obvious _____

4 a decrease _____

5 part of the film _____

6 not clear _____

7 given up _____

8 is attractive worldwide _____ _____

4 Write the verb in brackets in the correct form.

1 If we had a choice, I _____ (choose) product placement rather than a TV commercial.

2 If they _____ (have) more money, they'd ask a famous celebrity to endorse it.

3 It'd be cheaper if we _____ (give) out leaflets on the street.

4 If Sean Connery _____ (be) available, we'd hire him.

5 What _____ (happen) if we advertised on the radio?

6 If our cars _____ (have) our logo on the side, it would be a cheap form of advertising.

7 If you put your email on the site, we _____ (not/receive) so many phone calls.

8 I probably _____ (not/buy) it, even if it was half the price.

5 Complete each sentence in the first or the second conditional with the correct form of the verb in brackets.

1 Unless we spend more money on advertising, no one _will know_ (know) about our new product.

2 If I _____ (know) your email address, I would write to you, but I don't.

3 If you buy this one, you _____ (get) an extra one for free.

4 If I bought this one, _____ you _____ (give) me a two-year guarantee?

5 If you promote our product, we _____ (pay) you a million dollars.

6 What _____ (happen) to our sales if we used posters to advertise?

7 If we raise money for charity, it _____ (be) good for the company's image.

8 What _____ you _____ (do) if they don't buy your product any more?

VOCABULARY: word combinations

1 Combine a word in A with a word in B. Use these to complete sentences, 1–8.

A	B
advertising	message
junk	managers
media	analysis
fast	website
interactive	sums
persuasive	target
attractive	food
vast	food

(advertising is linked to managers)

1 _Advertising managers_ are becoming more and more interested in how to attract the child consumer.

2 Find out more information about the toys online at the store's own _____ _____ .

3 Advertisements with a _____ _____ tend to follow the formula of AIDA.

4 Now that there are more older people with spare time and cash, the 'grey consumer' has become a very _____ _____ for advertisers.

5 _____ _____ tells us that children influence 50 percent of what a family buys.

6 This is just _____ _____. It's full of fat, salt and sugar. Throw it away!

7 McDonald's and other _____ _____ restaurants are masters of advertising to children.

8 We've spent _____ _____ of money on TV commercials but I don't see any increase in sales!

GRAMMAR: comparison

2 Read this text about advertising controls. Write each adjective in brackets in the comparative or superlative form.

A new group of parents and politicians in the USA are now asking for [1] _____ (good) controls on 'junk food' adverts. The group describes these as the [2] _____ (worrying) type of advert because recent studies show US children are [3] _____ (fat) than ever before.

Another key request is to make TV advertising time [4] _____ (short) – from the current ten minutes per hour down to five minutes. The group also wants adverts for adults to be broadcast [5] _____ (late) in the day, when children are in bed.

While TV commercials might be one of the [6] _____ (effective) ways of reaching children, critics also say the situation is made [7] _____ (bad) because marketers are now reaching youngsters with an even [8] _____ (wide) range of media including the Internet, cellphones and video games.

And it isn't just at home where advertisers are being [9] _____ (persuasive) than ever. Companies can sponsor teams at school and use in-school advertising. As one parent said, 'we can tell our children to be [10] _____ (aware) of advertising but then our schools are giving them a completely different message!'

3 Read the first sentence and then complete the two sentences which follow with the correct forms of the adjective.

1 The first advert is funny. The second advert is really funny.

   a) The first advert isn't as _funny as_ the second advert.

   b) The second advert is _funnier than_ the first advert.

2 My country and Germany have the same laws on advertising to children. Sweden's laws are stricter.

   a) Sweden has the _____ laws of the three countries.

   b) Germany's laws are _____ my country's laws.

3 Drink X is tasty. Drink Y is tastier. Drink Z is as tasty as drink Y.

   a) Y and Z are _____ drinks.

   b) X isn't _____ Y and Z

LISTENING

LISTEN BETTER:

When you listen for specific information, read the questions first and try to predict the type of information you will be listening for. For example, if you are listening for a type of advert, think of some of the different types of advertising you know about.

4 `1.26` Listen to part of a meeting at an advertising agency. Complete the notes with the missing words.

The agency is planning a new ¹_____
_____ .

It will be shown during ²_____
_____ like ³_____

_____ .

The agency will also promote the company
by ⁴_____ _____

_____ _____ .

In the commercial they will use a famous soccer
player to ⁵_____ _____

_____ _____ of shoe.

He will wear the shoe which has the
⁶_____ _____

_____ _____ .

At the end of the advert the player will say
something about the product which
⁷_____ _____

_____ _____ .

PRONUNCIATION: weak forms

5a `1.27` When we speak, some words and syllables are 'weaker' than others. Weak vowels have this sound:

/ə/

Listen and mark the weak vowels in these sentences.

      /ə/   /ə/   /ə/
1 Mark's as tall as Michael.

2 Coffee tastes better than tea.

3 It's a lot faster.

4 We're sellers of soft drinks.

5 Is it as expensive?

5b `1.27` Listen again and practise saying the sentences.

DICTATION

6 `1.28` Look at this list of famous companies or brands. Listen to their slogans and write them down. All the slogans include a comparative or superlative form.

Philips Electronics:

_____

Duracell:

_____

Apple Computers:

_____

Pfizer pharmaceuticals:

_____

Country Life butter:

_____

Nescafe:

_____

Maltesers (chocolates):

_____

Disneyland:

_____

Dodge Trucks:

_____

KEY LANGUAGE: a presentation

1 Here are some typical phrases and sentences we use in presentations. Match each beginning, 1–10, with its correct ending, a–j.

1 Good morning everyone ____

2 I'd like to introduce my colleagues. ____

3 Our purpose today is to ____

4 I'm going to talk about ____

5 The presentation is divided into three parts. ____

6 If you have any questions, ____

7 Please look at the screen. ____

8 Now ____

9 So that brings us to the end of the presentation. I hope ____

10 Thank you very much for your attention. Are ____

a) the new slogan.

b) there any questions?

c) and thank you for coming.

d) let me summarise our main points.

e) First of all, this is Rachel Geiger who works in Marketing.

f) First, we'll be looking at the initial designs.

g) give our proposals for the new commercial.

h) you've found it informative.

i) Here you can see the schedule…

j) we'd be pleased to answer them at the end of the presentation.

2 [1.29] Listen to three extracts from the presentation. Tick the phrases or parts of phrases you hear from Exercise 1.

3 [1.29] Someone is making notes at the presentation but they have made some mistakes. Listen again and correct the notes.

Purpose of presentation

To present plans for the new advertising campaign on ~~TV~~ the Internet

Four parts to presentation:

— overview of the target market and websites

— presentation of slogans on new ads

— questions

Design of banner ads:

— the company colour will change

— the letters of the name won't change

— the logo will appear on some adverts

Costs

— Internet advertising is more expensive than TV in terms of production costs

— you need more time to find good sites for the adverts

— Internet advertising allows you to sell to customers more carefully

STUDY SKILLS: using your dictionary

1 Look at these entries from the Longman Active Study Dictionary. Use them to help you choose answers to questions 1–6.

> **commerce** /ˈkɒmɜːs $ ˈkɑːmɜːrs/ *n*
> [U] the activity of buying and selling things in business
>
> **commercial¹** /kəˈmɜːʃəl $ -ɜːr-/ *adj*
> relating to the buying and selling of things and with making money: *The film was a commercial success.*
> —**commercially** *adv*
>
> **commercial²** *n* [C] an advertisement on television or radio: *TV commercials* → see box at
> **ADVERTISEMENT**
>
> **commercialized** also **-ised** *BrE*
> /kəˈmɜːʃəlaɪzd $ -ɜːr-/ *adj disapproving*
> too concerned with making money:
> *The resort is too commercialized.*
> —**commercialism** *n* [U]

1 How many different words can be formed out of the word *commerce*?
a) Four   b) Five   c) Six

2 How many of these words are nouns?
a) three   b) four   c) two

3 What type of word is *commercially*?
a) adjective   b) adverb   c) noun

4 What is the reason for the mistake in this question:
How <s>many</s> *much* commercialism is there in your country?

a) Because commercialism is uncountable.

b) Because commercialism is countable.

c) Because commercialism is an adjective.

5 Which word can you use in front of *commercial*?
a) money   b) selling   c) TV

6 Which syllable is stressed in the word *commerce*?
a) first   b) second   c) third

7 Which syllable is stressed in the word *commercialized*?
a) first   b) second   c) third

8 Which noun is derived from *commercialized*?
a) commerce   b) commercialism
c) commercial

EXTRA VOCABULARY: dependent prepositions

2 Categorise these words with dependent prepositions in the correct column in the table.

look forward to

enquire about

show on

information about   succeed in

complain about   horrified by

problem with   complaint about

interested in

law against   apologise for

verb + preposition	adjective + preposition	noun + preposition
enquire about		

WRITING: a formal letter

3 These sentences are from formal letters. Use a phrase from the table to complete each sentence. Change the form of the verb where necessary.

1 I wish to <u>*enquire about*</u> the range of services you are able to offer. Please send details to…

2 I am writing to request more _____ a product I saw on your website.

3 I have recently watched the children's channel and I was _____ the level of violence in all the TV programmes for children.

4 I am surprised that you are prepared to _____ this kind of advertisement _____ television before most children are in bed.

5 I am writing to _____ the poor quality of service I received at one of your shops.

6 I recently purchased a laptop from you but there appears to be a _____ the modem.

7 I would like to _____ the delay in this delivery and any inconvenience you may have experienced.

8 I _____ hearing from you in the near future.

6 Business

6.1 IN BUSINESS

VOCABULARY: business terms, verb + noun combinations

1 Match each verb in A to a noun in B.

A	B
charge	your staff
make	low wages
make	high prices
pay	a profit
break	the law
avoid	a loss
invest	paying
value	in the local community

2 Complete each sentence with a verb + noun combination.

1 Before you start to *charge high prices* find out about your competitors' prices. They may be a lot lower.

2 In the first year you need to be prepared to _____ as you will have many costs.

3 To _____ tax is not recommended!

4 You should _____ because your workers are important for your business.

5 Once you are established, try to _____ . This will give you plenty of good publicity and a feeling of helping people.

6 It's always a bad idea to _____ as the government will find out in the end.

7 You could _____ but this might mean that you will lose staff.

8 Don't expect to _____ right from the start. It may be two or three years before you see any real financial reward.

3 Write the missing letters to complete these business roles.

1 If the costs go up, it will be the c _u_ s _t_ o _m_ e _r_ who ends up paying more.

2 My brother is a real e __ t __ e __ r __ n __ u __ . He can sell you anything.

3 Let me introduce you to my business p __ r __ n __ r.

4 R __ t __ i __ e __ s are complaining that deliveries of our goods are too slow.

5 Can you call the w __ o __ e __ a __ e __ and order five more?

6 The items were already damaged when they left the m __ n __ f __ c __ u __ e __ .

LISTENING

4 `2.2` A bank manager is talking to a customer who wants to borrow money to open a shop. Complete the bank manager's notes.

The premises consist of a (1) _____ on a street corner.

The client has some of the (2) _____ he needs. This includes some money from family members. He will also need to sell (3) _____ .

The bank needs to lend (4) _____ .

In the (5) _____ for his profit and losses, he plans to pay back about a (6) _____ a month.

I explained that both of his supermarket competitors are also the (7) _____ but he intends to offer lots of (8) _____ to (9) _____ .

READING

1 **Put each sentence, a–g, into the correct place to complete the text about PR managers.**

a) They were giving the water to people who were injured.

b) However, it took some years for the company to change this image.

c) He or she must defend a business when something goes wrong which may affect the company.

d) This is particularly true when tourism is destroyed in a country by a natural disaster.

e) So if journalists and the media find out any interesting news about their private lives it can also affect the company.

f) The way a company manufactures its products might attract criticism.

g) Problems with the people who work for you also often cause PR problems.

THE ROLE OF THE PUBLIC RELATIONS MANAGER

The job of the public relations manager is a difficult one. [1]____ So, if the press finds out the company is doing something unethical, for example, the PR manager will have to talk to journalists and convince customers that they have done nothing wrong. Here are the main things that the PR manager must look out for:

Acts of God

These are the things which no human can stop. For example, when the weather causes a crisis because of a hurricane or tornado, it may cause a PR disaster. [2]____ Many people remember the famous *tsunami* of 2005 which hit countries such as Thailand. PR managers were working day and night to save tourism.

Business Operations

[3]____ For example, if you had a factory which was putting chemicals or toxins into water and then the water was affecting the local area, you would need a highly-skilled PR manager. This person needs to make sure the general public doesn't stop buying the company's products.

Gossip and Rumours

Gossip and media rumours can really damage a company and affect the brand. Take the case of the international company which was accused of being evil. Some people said it was working with the 'Devil'! The gossip started with a competitor and was untrue. [4]____

Staff

[5]____ When New York's Twin Towers fell down on 9/11, a member of staff at a Starbucks Coffee House was charging emergency rescue workers for bottled water. [6]____ This story was passed around on the Internet and was highly damaging.

Scandal

Many celebrities often endorse a company's products. [7]____ Similarly, news about financial problems in the company will mean the PR department needs to get busy.

GRAMMAR: Past continuous

2 Underline the correct verb form, Past simple or Past continuous.

I ¹ *worked/was working* late one evening at my desk at home when I ² *noticed/was noticing* that my laptop computer ³ *became/was becoming* really hot. I ⁴ *switched/was switching* it off so it could cool down while I ⁵ *eat/was eating* my dinner.

Then, when I ⁶ *began/was beginning* to work again the computer did the same thing. I ⁷ *just wondered/ was just wondering* what to do when smoke started to come out of the back of the machine. I ⁸ *threw/was throwing* it out of the window into the swimming pool.

The next morning, while I ⁹ *tried/was trying* to telephone the manufacturer I ¹⁰ *saw/was seeing* on the TV news that the company ¹¹ *asked/was asking* people to return the laptops because the batteries ¹² *were/were being* dangerous!

3 Write the verbs in brackets in the past simple or past continuous form.

I couldn't believe it when I ¹ _____ (see) the offer. The company ² _____ (offer) free flights to customers who bought a vacuum cleaner from them. So the next day I ³ _____ (go) straight to my nearest electrical store. When I reached the shop, lots of other people ⁴ _____ (also/buy) vacuum cleaners to get their free tickets. Finally, I ⁵ _____ (buy) mine but after a week I ⁶ _____ (still/wait) for the tickets to arrive in the post. Then I ⁷ _____ (hear) on the news that the company had made a big mistake. Over 220,000 other people ⁸ _____ (also/wait) for their tickets. In the end lots of customers ⁹ _____ (take) the company to court and we all ¹⁰ _____ (get) our tickets. They say it was one of the greatest marketing disasters of all time.

PRONUNCIATION: weak forms

4a `2.3` Listen and write in the missing words.

1 _____ _____ busy when it rang.

2 _____ _____ in another part of the building.

3 _____ _____ with you?

4 He said _____ _____ .

5 _____ _____ waiting for us?

6 _____ _____ late as usual.

7 _____ _____ talking to someone.

8 Yes, _____ _____ .

4b `2.3` Listen again and underline the stressed words or syllables in each sentence. Practise saying the sentences.

DICTATION

5 `2.4` Listen to a news report about a problem with a product. Write in the missing words.

Here is the news. Today _____ _____ _____ after the US food safety authority said that customers had become ill _____ . At first the authority _____ _____ since May 2006. However, by last night _____ _____ with the product code 2111 were dangerous. Public relations representatives from the food company _____ . One manager said that _____ and _____ .

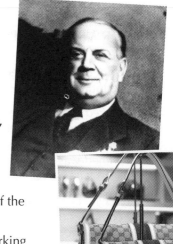

VOCABULARY: business words

1 Write in the missing word. The first letter is given.

1 Using the Internet, I can virtually r_____ the whole company from my home.

2 How much of a p_____ did you m_____ last year?

3 The next conference in Dubai will be a good moment to l_____ the new model.

4 My father tried to f_____ his first company with only a hundred dollars.

5 If sales keep falling like this, we'll go b_____ .

6 After six hours in the meeting we finally managed to n_____ a good contract.

7 Let's try and introduce this p_____ to an older type of customer who would never normally buy computer games.

TRANSLATION

2 Translate the sentences 1–7 in Exercise 1 into your language.

1 _____

_____

2 _____

_____

3 _____

_____

4 _____

_____

5 _____

_____

6 _____

_____

7 _____

_____

READING

3 Put the sentences in the correct order in this description of the history of the Italian fashion house, Gucci. Number them from 1 to 8.

Guccio Gucci (1881–1953)

____ He became president of the company in 1989.

____ After a few years of working for himself, he had built a reputation for his leather craftsmanship and accessories.

____ In 1953 the first overseas shop opened in New York City.

____ Following a series of legal and family problems, the company was sold off in 1993.

____ Gucci opened his first shop in Florence in 1920.

____ Later, Guccio's four sons helped him run the firm.

____ In the same year Guccio died and he never saw the Gucci empire spread around the world.

____ His grandson, Maurizio (1949–1995), took over the business in the 1980s and enjoyed great success.

4 ▣ 2.5 Listen and check your answers.

EXTRA VOCABULARY: word building

5 Complete this table with the correct forms of the words.

verb	noun	person
[1]manage	management	[2]manager
[3]	manufacturing	[4]
compete	[5]	[6]
[7]	[8]	employer
[9]	[10]	advertiser
[11]	supply	[12]

6 Complete sentences 1–12 with words from the table in Exercise 5.

1 My father is the _____ of a large company which produces furniture. He's worked there for over twenty years.

2 Many countries moved their _____ industries to Asia at the end of the last century and concentrated on service industries.

3 What _____ skills would you say you have? For example, are you good at organising teams of people?

4 I saw your _____ for sales staff in the local newspaper.

5 We'll need to _____ ten more people to work in the shop for the Christmas period.

6 It's important to know who your _____ are when you go into business. Find out what they offer and how you can be better than them.

7 Can you ring the _____ and order three more printers?

8 We _____ parts for cars at this factory.

9 The government's latest _____ figures show more people are in work than ever before.

10 Where do you think we should _____ our latest product?

11 They sell 90 percent of their goods in this country but they also _____ retailers in three other countries.

12 With over 30 factories in over twenty countries, they are probably the biggest _____ of sportswear in the world.

GRAMMAR: past perfect

7 Complete the information about the entrepreneur Alan Sugar. Choose the correct verb form, past simple, past perfect or past continuous.

SIR ALAN SUGAR (1947–)

The British entrepreneur (1) *was born/had been born* on 24 March, 1947. His father (2) *had been/was being* a tailor but after Sugar (3) *was leaving/had left* school aged 16, he (4) *started/had started* selling products like cigarette lighters and TV aerials. In 1968 he (5) *founded/had founded* a home electronics company called Amstrad and while he (6) *had launched/was launching* the new business, he married his wife, Ann.

His big success was with a home computer product in 1985. While other companies (7) *were selling/had sold* computers for over a £1,000 or more, Amstrad suddenly (8) *launched/had launched* a computer with cheap components for only £300. During the 1990s he (9) *had moved/moved* into other areas of business and now, with an estimated fortune of £760 million, he has his own TV show.

8 Write the verbs in brackets in the correct form, past perfect or past simple.

1 After we _____ (be) in business for a year, we made our first profit.

2 Before she _____ (start) this company, she'd worked for three years in the fashion industry.

3 The company _____ (close) in 2005.

4 They _____ (plan) to launch the new software before last October, but problems delayed the official launch date.

5 By the time he celebrated his twenty-first birthday he _____ (make) his first million and he then _____ (go) on to create a worldwide brand.

KEY LANGUAGE: negotiating

1 [2.6] A supplier in the USA is calling a company in Italy. Listen to the telephone conversation and answer the questions.

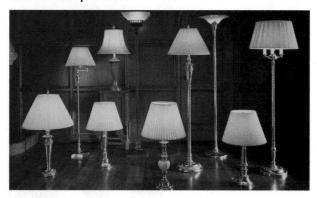

1 Where is the caller based?

_____

2 Where did he find out about Prima's products?

_____

3 What kind of company does the caller work for?

_____

4 What is he particularly interested in?

_____

5 How many does he want?

_____

6 Why is that a problem?

_____

7 What is the advantage of ordering a large amount?

_____

8 What does the caller offer?

_____

2a One word is missing from each sentence. Write it in.

1 How many ∧ *would* you like to order?

2 We are thinking placing a large order.

3 I'm afraid would be a bit difficult.

4 What about we paid earlier?

5 How you feel about that?

6 Let check if I understand you.

7 Would you able to do that?

8 That fine.

2b [2.6] Listen to the telephone call again and check your answers.

PRONUNCIATION EXTRA: stressing a key word

3a [2.7] Sometimes we stress one word in a phrase to add emphasis. Listen to the phrases below and underline the word or syllable with the main stress.

1 I'm af<u>raid</u> he's out.

2 That will be really difficult for us.

3 We're thinking of placing a large order.

4 That sounds great!

5 I'm so sorry but I can't.

6 How many would you like?

7 Did you say a hundred?

8 Can you deliver by tomorrow?

3b [2.7] Listen again and practise saying the sentences.

4 Read the clues and write the words in the table.

1 This is the amount you want.

2 The noun form of 'to pay'.

3 Something that's at a much lower price than normal.

4 The supplier gives you this when you get 10% off the normal price.

5 Everyone wants to 'make' this with money.

6 This refers to how the goods arrive and by when.

7 If this is wide, your customers will appreciate the choice.

8 This person sells the goods.

9 You need to 'place' this with the supplier.

				N			
	2			E			
		3		G			
		4		O			
5				T			
		6		I			
			7	A			
		8		T			
		9		E			

STUDY SKILLS: formal and informal language

1 Match the formal words, 1–8 to the less formal words a–h with the same meaning.

1	enquire	**a)**	can't
2	inform	**b)**	want
3	delighted	**c)**	ask about
4	am unable	**d)**	happy
5	wish	**e)**	sorry
6	apologise	**f)**	tell
7	assistance	**g)**	ask
8	request	**h)**	help

2 Here are two emails, one formal and one informal. They are mixed up. Separate the emails and write them in the correct order.

I would be delighted to meet you next week.

See you there.

Shall I bring anything?

~~Dear Mr Smith~~

All the best

With reference to your previous email…

Good to hear from you.

Hi Jake

Yours sincerely

The party sounds great – I'd love to come.

If you wish, I would also be happy to give you a tour of the factory.

I look forward to seeing you.

1	_Dear Mr Smith_
2	
3	
4	
5	
6	

a	
b	
c	
d	
e	
f	

WRITING: emails

WRITE BETTER

If you want to write an email but you don't know how formal you should be, think about:

- Who the email is to? (How well do you know them?)
- How formal was their last email to you? Write back in a similar style.
- If it's the first time you have written to someone, be safe and write more formally rather than less formally.

3 The email below is too informal. Rewrite it using more formal language.

Hi customer!

1 _Dear customer_

Just a quick email to tell you about a change on our website

2

It's great news because now you can order online.

3

Could you possibly register within the next two weeks?

4

Email me back if you need any help with this.

5

Speak to you soon.

6

All the best.

7

7 Design

7.1 DESIGN IS EVERYWHERE

1 Use a form of the word in bold to complete sentences 1–10.

design

1 He works as a _____ for an engineering firm.

science

2 Einstein probably made the biggest _____ breakthrough of the last hundred years.

manufacture

3 We're the largest _____ of paint in Europe.

produce

4 Let's stop now. That was a very _____ meeting.

use

5 This website is very _____-friendly.

develop

6 Have you seen that new housing _____? It's so ugly.

innovate

7 To solve this problem I need you to come up with some really new and _____ ideas.

invent

8 His latest _____ is a car which runs on air!

art

9 Michelangelo is the _____ everybody has heard of.

engine

10 I'm an _____ for an oil company.

2 Match an adjective from the box to the pictures.

futuristic   elegant   mass-produced
streamlined   ~~traditional~~   retro
hand-made   innovative

1   _traditional_

2   _____

3   _____

4   _____

5   _____

6   _____

7   _____

8   _____

VOCABULARY: abstract nouns

1 Write the correct ending to complete these abstract nouns.

1 Streamli*ning* originally evolved through the design of boats and aircraft.

2 The bright colours and shapes in design were a response to the new opti_____ in the country after the war.

3 The old traditions and styles were replaced with the need for moderni_____ in design.

4 Television advertising was partly responsible for mass consume_____ .

5 For many years people didn't realise the damage done to the environment by industrialis_____ .

6 Greater efficien_____ in this factory would help to reduce the costs.

7 Ergono_____ is the study of the ways in which a design can be made easier to use.

8 Recy_____ is one major factor affecting modern designs and consumer taste.

9 Designers need to keep up with the latest technological innova_____ .

PRONUNCIATION

2a 2.8 Listen to six of the abstract nouns in Exercise 1. Which syllable is stressed? Tick the correct stress pattern below.

1 o o O	o O o	O o o ✓
2 O o o o	o o o O	o O o o
3 o O o o	o o O o	O o o o
4 o o o O o	O o o o o	o O o o o
5 O o O o o	o o O o O o o	o O o o o O o
6 o o o O	o O o o	O o o o

2b 2.8 Listen again and practise saying the words.

LISTENING

3a 2.9 Listen to three designers discussing ideas and answer the questions.

1 What kind of device are they talking about?

_____

2 Which materials have they mentioned?

_____

3 What different shapes have they discussed?

_____

4 Why should they test different versions?

_____

5 When is the launch?

_____

3b 2.9 Listen again and complete the notes from their meeting?

Notes on new design for music player:
Everyone agreed that it will be:
(1) very _____ so it won't break while people are carrying it around.
(2) not made of _____ because it's too heavy.
(3) made of _____ and in lots of different colours.
There was disagreement over the (4) _____ :
if it is rectangular it might look like all the competitors' (5) _____ but on the other hand customers can easily put it in their (6) _____ .
Action plan:
Make a few (7) _____ and test them on consumers. (Note that we will need to check if there's enough time for testing before the (8) _____ next spring.)

GRAMMAR: modals

4 **Look at these pairs of sentences. Choose from the phrases below to complete sentence b with the same meaning as sentence a.**

's possibly

isn't advisable

's possible

isn't possible

's important

's advisable

's essential

aren't able

1   a) This new kind of material could be useful for all sorts of things.

   b) This new kind of material *'s possibly* useful for all sorts of things.

2   a) We can't use toxic chemicals.

   b) We _____ to use toxic chemicals.

3   a) I think we should make them in pink.

   b) It _____ to make them in pink.

4   a) The shape has to be smooth.

   b) It _____ that the shape is smooth.

5   a) In my opinion, it must be user-friendly if we want people to buy it.

   b) In my opinion, it _____ that it's user-friendly so people will buy it.

6   a) We shouldn't use any chemicals.

   b) It _____ to use any chemicals.

7   a) It couldn't break, could it?

   b) It _____ for it to break, is it?

8   a) We should test them on customers.

   b) It _____ to test them on customers.

9   a) We can't sell them unless it is the right product.

   b) We _____ to sell them unless it is the right product.

10 a) We can test them on our staff.

   b) It _____ to test them on our staff.

5a **Choose the correct modal verb from 1–10, a, b or c, to complete each gap in the following discussion.**

A: The material for this ¹ __a__ be very strong. We don't want it to break while people are carrying it around.

B: That's right. We ² _____ use metal because it's too heavy.

C: Yes I agree. If we use a strong plastic, we ³ _____ make it in lots of different colours and it's also possible to make a rectangular shape.

A: Why rectangular? It ⁴ _____ look like all the competitors' designs, does it? I think we ⁵ _____ try to come up with something new. We ⁶ _____ make circular players, for example, or star-shaped players.

B: True, but we ⁷ _____ produce something which people ⁸ _____ easily carry. The classic rectangular shape works because it's easy to put in your pocket.

C: Well, we ⁹ _____ design a few versions and test them on consumers.

A: No, we can't because we don't have enough time before the launch next spring.

B: I know, but we ¹⁰ _____ launch it until we're ready otherwise it won't sell.

1 a) must	b) can	c) doesn't have to
2 a) don't have to	b) shouldn't	c) couldn't
3 a) have to	b) must	c) can
4 a) doesn't have to	b) mustn't	c) shouldn't
5 a) should	b) don't have to	c) have
6 a) couldn't	b) must	c) could
7 a) don't have to	b) mustn't	c) couldn't
8 a) can't	b) can	c) have to
9 a) have to	b) must	c) can
10 a) should	b) shouldn't	c) couldn't

5b `2.9` **Now listen again and check your answers.**

GRAMMAR: present deduction

1 Match a phrase 1–6 to each picture a–f.

1 It must be fast!

2 It can't be real.

3 This can't be mine!

4 She might be feeling ill.

5 That could be dangerous.

6 It must be a Picasso.

a) _____

b) _____

c) _____

d) _____

e) _____

f) _____

2 Look at these pairs of sentences. Choose from the words below to complete sentence B with the same meaning as sentence A. There is one extra word.

can	perhaps	not possible	must	must
can't	can't	certain	might	

1 A This is definitely one of the classic designs of the last century.

   B This _____ be one of the classic designs of the last century.

2 A She can't be in the office. No-one has seen her.

   B It's _____ that she's in the office.

3 A I'm sure this isn't the latest model.

   B This _____ be the latest model.

4 A Maybe it's an original, but I'm not certain.

   B It _____ be an original.

5 A This design isn't by da Vinci because it's from the seventeenth century.

   B This design _____ be by da Vinci because it's from the seventeenth century.

6 A I'm sure she's feeling tired.

   B She _____ be feeling tired.

7 A They could be in a meeting.

   B _____ they're in a meeting.

8 A Rona must be having a few days' holiday.

   B I'm _____ Rona is having a few days' holiday.

DICTATION

3 [2.10] Listen to a short lecture on design in the twentieth century. Write the missing words.

_____ in design began in the nineteen thirties. _____ increased the _____ of transport and this influenced the _____ .
Consumers wanted _____ .
Later in the sixties, _____
_____
of the period and the rise of the throwaway society.
The period saw _____
_____
_____
_____ and design. Later in the century, there was a reaction against the throwaway culture and _____ .
Designers knew they _____
and products with a focus on durability.

READING

READ BETTER

To help you, first read all the questions, then ALL the text and look for the answers to the questions.

4 Read about three innovations in design. Match one design, A, B, or C, to each question, 1–10.

GREEN DESIGNS OF THE YEAR!

At Eco-home magazine we must see hundreds of great innovations every year but we can't give prizes to all of them. After days of discussion, here are the top three for this year.

According to the article, which innovation

1 uses no chemicals? ____

2 uses very few chemicals? ____

3 helps you breathe more easily? ____

4 is comfortable to sit on? ____

5 looks like other similar designs? ____

6 can make many other objects? ____

7 might you walk on? ____

8 might you walk in? ____

9 is produced in a place that is also environmentally friendly? ____

10 was designed for something else? ____

DESIGN A: Most innovative furniture of the year

The winner in this category was Zelfo Australia's Peanut Chair. It is made 100 percent from plant material with no glue, so it cares for the environment as well as the owner. Zelfo is the name of the company and the name of the material they use to make all their products. The material combines plants and paper and provides an alternative to the chemicals and plastics in most types of furniture. Zelfo uses no chemicals and its factory in Australia recycles as much of its water as possible, with no toxic waste. Zelfo is also currently used in the production of musical instruments and toys. You might even be wearing their sunglasses in the future!

DESIGN B: Best innovation in houses

If you walk through the area of Segrate in Milan you could find that the air smells fresher than in most other cities. That's because the road in the city centre is covered in concrete which cleans the air. Italy's largest cement maker, Italcementi first discovered the cement when it made a concrete for a new church in Rome. The idea was to design a chemical to keep the cement clean. They discovered that it could also clean the air around it. The company is certain that if 15 percent of all buildings had this cement, air pollution could fall by 50 percent.

DESIGN C: Design Team of the Year

Eco-home's final award goes to *Nike's Considered* team. As a sub-group of Nike, the aim of the team is to create an athlete's shoe which uses less energy, produces less waste, and is made with fewer chemicals. Its latest shoe *The Soaker* is an environmentally-friendly shoe but still with classic Nike design. It also contains 95 percent fewer chemicals than many other athletes' shoes.

KEY LANGUAGE: describing qualities

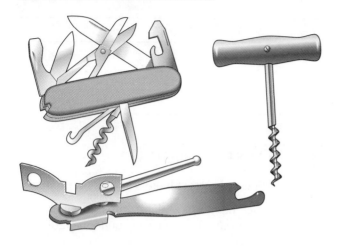

1a The speaker is introducing a new product. Put the presentation in order from 1 to 7. Which product is the speaker describing?

____ Today I'd like to present this new design.

____ However, the elegant handle is made completely of metal.

____ Good morning everyone and thanks for coming.

____ Because of this, one of the best points is that it's unlikely to break when you use it.

____ I'd expect that it would appeal to anyone who enjoys a glass of wine with their dinner.

____ At £5.50 it's excellent value for money and…

____ As you can see it looks very similar to the old wooden design.

1b `2.11` Listen and check your answers.

PRONUNCIATION: stressing words for emphasis

2a `2.12` Listen to these sentences and underline the stressed words or syllables.

1 It looks very stylish.

2 It has several qualities.

3 That's a special feature.

4 It has a metallic base.

5 It's excellent value for money.

6 It's made of a strong plastic.

2b `2.12` Listen again and practise saying the sentences

EXTRA VOCABULARY: describing shapes

3 Match the correct description to each shape.

> triangle   circle   square
> sphere   rectangle   cube

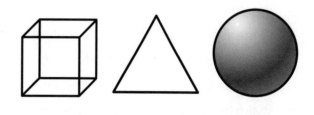

_____   _____   _____

_____   _____   _____

4 Write the correct adjective for each of the shape nouns in Exercise 3.

1 triangle (n) – _triangular_ (adj)

2 circle (n) – _____ (adj)

3 square (n) – _____ (adj)

4 rectangle (n) – _____ (adj)

5 cube (n) – _____ (adj)

6 sphere (n) – _____ (adj)

5 Now use one of the adjectives in each of these sentences.

1 It has a _____ point which writes on the paper.

2 The area is one hundred _____ metres in total.

3 It was a long time before the first people discovered that a _____ shape would be useful. Nowadays, it's hard to imagine life without the wheel!

4 There's a small _____ wooden box on my desk which has pens in it.

5 The measurements of the box are 3 cm x 3 cm x 3cm. So it's 27 _____ centimetres in total.

6 Football in England uses a _____ ball but a football in the USA is a different shape.

STUDY SKILLS: editing and proofreading

1 Read this email and correct ten mistakes. There is one mistake in each line.

D

1 ~~dear~~ Ray

2 I write about the attachment you sent with

3 the two desines. I really like the first one

4 which is made of wood. It looks like very

5 stylish but not very functional the second

6 might to be better because it's easy to use but

7 it isn't very inovative. How about combining

8 the appearance of first and the practicality of

9 the second? Please sending me your new

10 design by thursday.

Natalie.

TRANSLATION

2 Translate the corrected email in Exercise 1 into your language.

WRITING: a report

3 Underline the correct linkers in these sentences.

1 You can set the morning alarm with this switch. *Also/As a result* it lets you wake up to the radio if you want.

2 The price is very competitive at £120. *Although/Consequently* it will be attractive to a wide market.

3 It only comes in black so it looks rather boring. *On the other hand/Moreover* it's very light and easy to carry.

4 Everything is automatic so the owner doesn't need to touch anything. *However/As a result* it's easy for anyone to use.

5 The battery lasts for six hours. *Moreover/consequently,* it only takes about one hour to fully recharge.

6 *Although/Also* it has a traditional appearance, the technology inside is the most up-to-date on the market.

4 Write a suitable linking word or phrase in each space to complete this paragraph from a report about two laptop computers.

1 _____ there are a number of similarities between the two models, the X920 is far more stylish than the Zastra001. 2 _____ , it is 2kg and 3 _____ much lighter than the Zastra001 which is 3.9kg. 4 _____ the Zastra has longer battery life and 5 _____ has a built-in webcam. 6 _____ , I would strongly recommend the X920 for our purposes.

8 Education

8.1 EDUCATION ISSUES

VOCABULARY: education

1 Write in the missing words. The first letter is given.

1 C_____ education is when you have to go to school.

2 You pay fees for p_____ education.

3 H_____ education allows you to continue studying when you leave school.

4 A child's first school is called p_____ school.

5 C_____ assessment is a technique for monitoring a student's progress over a long period.

6 Children are aged between 11–16 at
s_____ school in the UK.

7 N_____ or kindergarten is where children go before they start school.

TRANSLATION

2 Translate 1–7 in Exercise 1 into the equivalent terms for education in your country.

1 _____

2 _____

3 _____

4 _____

5 _____

6 _____

7 _____

VOCABULARY: studying

3 Match the two halves, 1–6 with a–f, to complete the sentences.

1 I didn't get ____

2 My teacher says I have to retake ____

3 We have to hand ____

4 She never makes ____

5 As long as you do ____

6 I stayed up all night revising ____

a) your best, that's all that matters.

b) in the essay today.

c) the place at the university I wanted.

d) for today's test.

e) mistakes.

f) the whole course!

4 Complete the gaps in the article about single sex education with the correct word, a, b or c.

SINGLE SEX SCHOOLING HELPS GIRLS LATER IN LIFE

Educational researchers have studied 13,000 females born in 1958. They looked at girls who ¹___ to single and mixed-sex schools and found that girls who ²___ at single-sex schools are more likely to ³___ traditionally male subjects such as maths and physics. This helps them to ⁴___ jobs in typically male-dominated professions. In fact, when both boys and girls were ⁵___ separately they were more likely to ⁶ ___ courses not normally associated with their sex. However, there was no evidence that girls in single-sex schools ⁷___ more progress academically.

1	a) went	b) took	c) learnt
2	a) taught	b) made	c) studied
3	a) take	b) revise	c) fail
4	a) apply	b) get	c) make
5	a) handed in	b) graduated	c) taught
6	a) revise	b) teach	c) do
7	a) did	b) made	c) got

VOCABULARY: words from the lesson

1 Underline the correct word.

1 Our teacher has a very *friendly/unfriendly* approach to the class. Everyone feels relaxed in his lessons.

2 The class has a very *outgoing/easy-going* atmosphere. The students were all smiling and joking.

3 I remember a maths teacher who used to make you stand if you made a mistake. He was very *strict/informal*.

4 Anyone in my class who isn't *punctual/informal* in the morning will have to stay one hour extra after school.

5 Our teacher always comes to class *strict/well-prepared*. She must spend hours planning her lessons.

6 I never get bored in my English classes. The teacher is interesting and the lessons have a fast *speed/pace*.

7 Her approach to learning is probably *common/unique*. I don't know anyone who does anything like it.

8 Children should be given positive encouragement rather than *criticised/complimented*.

2 Complete the sentences with words or phrases from the lesson. The first letter is given.

1 E_____ e_____ is the first 6 or 8 years of children's education.

2 You have h_____
e_____ at a college or university rather than a school.

3 Most institutions nowadays prefer
c_____ a_____ to mid-year exams to assess students' progress.

4 As a precaution against the violence among young people, we should increase the years of
c_____ e_____

5 There are wonderful job opportunities for science
g_____ .

6 His score is under average so the examination board has f_____ him.

READING

3 Read the article and complete this summary. Use words from the article.

Pott Row First School has given every [1]_____ a [2]_____ so that they can have their [3]_____ outside. This is because the [4]_____ believe that the children [5]_____ better and work harder in the [6]_____ . Both [7]_____ and [8]_____ think it is a good idea and the children are much [9]_____ and more [10]_____ about school.

OUTDOOR LESSONS TO HELP LEARNING

A primary school has given its pupils 'all-weather' school uniforms so they can have lessons outside, even in the rain. Pott Row First School wants to provide half of all lessons outside in the next two years.

The headteacher, Michelle Petzer, said the idea began when her teachers noticed that the children found it easier to concentrate out in the fresh air. 'We realised the children worked much better and were happier if they had been outside during the day,' she said. Staff would comment that if the children hadn't been outside, perhaps because it had been raining, they wouldn't listen so well in class.

'We realised that it is essential for the pupils to have the opportunity to play outdoors no matter what the weather conditions. As a result we have purchased raincoats for every single pupil in our school.'

Mrs Petzer said staff and parents had been extremely supportive of the idea. 'A number of parents have said how much happier their child is and how they are so enthusiastic about coming to school,' she said.

GRAMMAR: defining relative clauses

4 Write the missing relative pronouns in 1–5.

1 All students are individuals _____ need special attention.

2 Maths is a subject _____ is often difficult for many people.

3 Maria Montessori is someone _____ ideas have had a huge influence on modern education.

4 This is the university _____ I got my degree.

5 In my country most people graduate _____ they are about 21 or 22 years old.

5 Combine the two sentences using the relative pronoun in bold.

1 He's a professor. He works at a university in London.

who

He's a professor who works at a university in London.

2 Exams are a requirement. They take place every summer.

which

_____

_____

3 A teacher is a person. His or her job is to show students how to learn, as well as what to learn.

whose

_____

_____

4 The mid-morning break is a period in the school day. Pupils relax and change classrooms.

when

_____

_____

5 Grades are marks. They are often given for homework.

that

_____

_____

6 Nursery is a kind of playschool. Children aged 1–5 go there.

where

_____

_____

6 Which sentences don't need a relative pronoun? Which sentences must have a relative pronoun? Write a pronoun if necessary.

1 Students ∧ miss school sometimes fail their exams.
       who

2 The school I study at is a mixed-sex school.

3 Speak to the teacher is in charge of sports.

4 Children read with their parents for 30 minutes a day at home do very well at school.

5 This isn't the homework I did.

6 The bag I left in the classroom is brown.

PRONUNCIATION

7a [2.13] Read these words. Which word or underlined syllable has a different vowel sound?

1 a) do
  b) go ✓
  c) true
  d) who

2 a) <u>friend</u>ly
  b) when
  c) test
  d) real

3 a) late
  b) fact
  c) grade
  d) pace

4 a) re<u>vise</u>
  b) <u>pri</u>mary
  c) time
  d) paid

5 a) mixed
  b) <u>single</u>
  c) life
  d) strict

6 a) ex<u>am</u>
  b) than
  c) re<u>take</u>
  d) an

7 a) where
  b) air
  c) pre<u>pared</u>
  d) uni<u>ver</u>sity

8 a) teach
  b) de<u>gree</u>
  c) <u>the</u>sis
  d) when

7b [2.13] Now listen and check your answers. Listen again and practise saying the words.

READING

1 Complete each part of the reading about distance learning with a heading (a–f) below. There is one extra and incorrect heading.

a) Distance learning credits don't transfer to other colleges.

b) Online schools are faster and easier than traditional schools.

c) Distance learning schools aren't as good as traditional schools.

d) Distance learning is cheaper than traditional learning.

e) Accredited schools always offer a good education.

f) Employers won't accept degrees from distance learning universities.

2 Find a word in the text which means the same as the following:

1 A common but untrue belief: ___myth___

2 Something that looks genuine but isn't: _____

3 Officially recognised or approved (school): _____

4 Fast or speeded up: _____

5 The ability to change: _____

6 Communicate with: _____

3 Read the text again and decide if these statements are true or false.

1 The courses at many online universities are equal to any traditional university. ____

2 Employers actually prefer degrees from online universities. ____

3 Qualifications from schools which are officially approved won't necessarily mean much to anyone. ____

4 Make sure your course is with a recognised educational body. ____

5 The main benefit of online learning is that it can fit your way of working and requirements. ____

The Five Myths of Distance Learning

Myth 1: _____

Online universities can offer as good an education as any traditional school. You just have to choose the right online course. Many of these now allow students to interact with expert teachers and learn through the Internet.

Myth 2: _____

While this may be true of cheap schools or 'fake' schools, degrees from properly accredited schools are accepted by employers in the same way that traditional degrees are accepted.

Myth 3: _____

Qualifications from accredited online schools will be accepted by traditional institutions in the same way that grades and qualifications from 'regular' colleges are accepted.

Myth 4: _____

Anyone can claim to be an accredited agency, and many do. However, in order to be widely accepted, your degree needs to come from a college approved by your country's educational bodies. Always check with them first to avoid studying for an unrecognised qualification.

Myth 5: _____

While some online students choose accelerated courses, others select online schools that let them do their work slowly, over a longer period of time. Just like traditional schools, some online institutions are known for being easier and others are known for being harder. Flexibility is key in the world of distance learning and the majority of online courses can change to fit your needs.

GRAMMAR: relative clauses

4 Choose a relative clause, a–g, to add extra information to each sentence. See the first example.

1 Online universities, __d)__ can offer as good an education as any traditional school.

2 On the Internet, students can interact with expert teachers ____ .

3 Students often choose online courses, ____ and they can choose to work quickly or slowly.

4 Students ____ often prefer online learning to face-to-face learning.

5 Many online courses also have message boards and forums, ____ as well as having video lectures.

6 Online learning, ____ is now considered to be equal to face-to-face learning.

7 Ellie Hathaway, ____ says that she enjoyed it more than the traditional type of course.

a) which offer greater flexibility,

b) where you can interact with other online learners,

c) whose jobs prevent them from travelling to lectures,

d) ~~which are run via the Internet,~~

e) which in the past was regarded as poor quality education,

f) who are highly qualified

g) who recently completed an online course,

WRITE BETTER

Add relative clauses to your writing to make it more interesting. For example, look at how you can make this sentence more interesting for the reader:

'The house was on the hill.' ⟶

'The house, *which many people said was evil*, was on the hill.'

5 Rewrite these sentences with relative clauses to make them interesting.

1 The dog was black.

_____ .

2 The man was 68 years old.

_____ .

3 The school was outside the town.

_____ .

4 My old maths teacher was called Mr Smith.

_____ .

5 The classroom had 30 desks.

_____ .

6 The house is at the end of the road.

_____ .

7 The film was interesting.

_____ .

PRONUNCIATION

6 Put the missing commas in these sentences.

1 My school ⋏ which won an award last year ⋏ is a secondary school.

2 Mr Sanders who runs the maths department is my favourite teacher.

3 The library which was built in 1808 has over 50,000 books.

4 My university which is one of the most modern in the country is famous for science and research.

5 The students who were demonstrating against the Government cuts in education walked peacefully through the city centre.

7a [2.14] Listen to each sentence and notice where the speaker pauses. For example:

My school / which won an award last year / is a secondary school.

7b [2.14] Listen again and practise saying the sentences with the pauses.

SCENARIO: Trouble at lakeside

EXTRA VOCABULARY: describing facilities

1 Write the correct word or phrase in each sentence 1–7.

spacious	well-stocked	break down
standard	state-of-the-art	~~outstanding~~
well run		

1 This college has __*outstanding*__ teachers who all have degrees from famous universities.

2 It's a _____ library with all the books you need.

3 These classrooms are very _____ with plenty of room.

4 How often do the computers _____ ?

5 This is our _____ multimedia centre. It was installed just last month.

6 The teaching is good, but administratively the college isn't _____ .

7 The _____ of lecturing doesn't seem as high as the brochure claims.

DICTATION

2 **2.15** Listen to this advertisement for a college. Write in the missing words.

Where are you thinking of studying this year? Come to Riverside College _____

_____

_____ . Our 99 percent pass rate,

_____

_____ ,

_____ in the country. You'll

be amazed _____

time. You'll enjoy _____

_____ and _____

_____ media facilities.

And _____

there's our _____

_____ . Call us now on _____

_____ for a free brochure or _____

_____ .

KEY LANGUAGE: discussing possibilities and options

3 Complete each sentence with one of these words.

| way | what | now | advantage | ways |
| things | thing | options | | |

1 There are several _____ of dealing with this.

2 We have a number of _____ to choose from.

3 The _____ of this solution is that it's fair for everyone.

4 Let's see, what other _____ can we do?

5 The best _____ forward is to ask everyone what they think.

6 Deciding _____ to do next is important.

7 So, the next _____ to do is improve the computers.

8 What we've got to do _____ is restock the library.

4 Complete the dialogue with five of the sentences in Exercise 3.

A: So I've looked at the student feedback on these survey forms. I see that everyone was critical about the library.

B: Yes, it's clear that ¹_____

_____ .

A: I agree. Then there's the issue of the remarks about a certain teacher.

B: It's a problem and ²_____

_____ . One way is to question him first about the comments or perhaps we should observe one of his lessons.

A: I think observe him first. ³_____

_____ involved.

B: Right. I'll arrange to go into the lesson next week. The views about the self-access centre weren't bad.

A: No, students seem happy with access to newspapers, books and so on. Though there were a few complaints about the computers.

B: Yes, well, I agree that they are all old.

A: ⁴_____ .

B: Yes, to do that and find a better Internet provider. I'm not at all happy with our current service.

A: What about this last point on the survey about tutorials? Over half the students have requested more individual time with their personal tutors.

B: Yes, I saw that. Well, we can't do much about it until the next staff meeting. And I think ⁵_____ .

It's quite possible that the tutors will agree without any disagreement.

STUDY SKILLS: reading strategies

1 Match the terms *skimming* and *scanning* to these definitions.

a _____ is reading in order to find key words or specific points in the text

b _____ is reading to get the general idea of a text.

2 Look back at the text about distance learning on page 56 and answer the following:

Skimming:

1 How many myths are there?

2 What does the text compare?

3 Is the author arguing for or against this type of learning?

Scanning:

4 What is true of 'fake' schools?

5 What is key in the world of distance learning?

6 Who should you check with to find out if a degree is approved?

WRITING: a formal letter

3 Replace the 12 less formal words in the letter with these formal words. Write the informal word next to it.

1 enquiring _____

2 comprehensive _____

3 hesitate _____

4 enrol _____

5 Yours sincerely _____

6 further _____

7 delighted _____

8 Dear _____

9 are grateful _____

10 choose _____

11 enclosed _____

12 suitable _____

Hi Mrs Adamson

We thank you for your letter asking about our courses. I am happy to send you this year's brochure with full details of our summer programme.

As you will see from our brochure, we have over one hundred courses for you to pick from and feel sure you will find something good for you. Please take time to read all course descriptions and note the timetables and course lengths summarised at the back. Details of fees are also put inside.

If you wish to sign up, please note that you can now do so at our website: www.summerschools.com/enrolments

Should you need any more information about our courses, please don't wait to contact me. We look forward to hearing from you.

Best wishes

Lorna Haycroft

School Administrator

4 Use formal words and phrases from the letter in Exercise 3 to complete this reply.

¹ *Dear* Ms Haycroft.

I am ²_____ your brochure which arrived this morning. I found it very ³_____ and full of useful information.

⁴_____ see I have

⁵_____ an enrolment form for the arts and crafts course along with a cheque for the full ⁶_____ of £600.

⁷_____ note that I would also like accommodation during the course, so I am requesting details of somewhere ⁸_____ for me in the town.

⁹_____ need to discuss accommodation with me, please do not ¹⁰_____ to telephone me on 01867 564 7384 during the day.

¹¹_____

from you and taking the course this summer.

¹²_____ regards

Rita Adamson.

9 Engineering

9.1 FROM ENGINES TO ENGINEERS

1 Choose one type of engineering to match the inventions listed in 1–5.

> biomedical   computer   aerospace   ~~civil~~
> mechanical

1 Railways, roads, bridges = _____civil_____ engineering.

2 Spacecraft, satellites, missiles = _____ engineering.

3 MRI scanners, heart pacemakers, artificial limbs = _____ engineering.

4 Cars, CD players, washing machines = _____ engineering.

5 Microchips, robots, networks = _____ engineering.

TRANSLATION

2 Translate the different types of engineering and inventions in Exercise 1 into your language.

1 _____

2 _____

3 _____

4 _____

5 _____

LISTENING

3 2.16 A student is talking to a careers advisor. Listen and complete the student's notes below.

> The term ¹_____ can mean different things.
> ²_____ engineering includes areas such as aerospace, the
> ³_____ or things for
> ⁴_____ .
> ⁵_____ engineers find ways to stop ⁶_____ from factories or how to ⁷_____ after an oil spill in the ocean.
> Engineers like ⁸_____ and are ⁹_____ new things.

VOCABULARY: word combinations

4 Match the first half 1–8 with the second half a–h of these sentences.

1 I'd like to test ___

2 I'm afraid we couldn't find ___

3 Without doing some ___

4 It shouldn't be much longer before they've built ___

5 They say they've made ___

6 They haven't met one single ___

7 Maybe we could solve ___

8 He's doing his ___

a) tests it's impossible to know if it's safe.

b) a major breakthrough.

c) the problem with a new version.

d) us a prototype.

e) deadline since we started.

f) a solution.

g) research into nanotechnology.

h) your theory with this experiment.

A ROLLERCOASTER OF A JOB

The year after the rollercoaster ride Big Thunder was opened at the Disneyland Resort in Paris, its inventor Mike Kent rode it 400 times. Not only does he enjoy his own rides, it also shows how confident he is in the safety of his own engineering. (1)____

Mike is an attractions engineer at the resort. He was first employed by Disney in 1990. 'The advert asked for an engineer with a touch of magic,' he remembers. (2)____ He left college to work in the petrochemical industry. After that he was also asked to work in the aerospace industry and by the car firm Rolls Royce.

As well as taking unlimited rides at Disneyland, the attraction of the job was the freedom: 'You are one big team. In my previous job I was always being told, "That's not your job". (3)____ There's a huge amount of creativity.'

Now, the Big Thunder ride can be enjoyed at every Disney resort in the world and that gives Kent a great deal of satisfaction: 'The day we opened Big Thunder to the public I was watching. (4)____ Everyone in the train applauded. Normally when you design something you don't get a round of applause for it', or screams of fear and delight!

READING

1 Complete each gap, 1–4, in the article with a sentence from a–e. There is one extra sentence.

a) The first train went out and came back.

b) Up to this point, his career had been quite varied.

c) And he should be because he designed the ride.

d) Mike always wanted to work in this type of engineering.

e) No one here has ever said that.

2 Answer questions 1–5 about Mike Kent. Choose your answer from a, b or c.

1 The writer thinks Mike Kent

   a) only rides Big Thunder to test it.

   b) enjoys it as much as the average person.

   c) is much more than an average rollercoaster rider.

2 According to the article, what is the other reason he takes so many rides on Big Thunder?

   a) He doesn't think it is dangerous.

   b) He needs to test it.

   c) It helps him to design it.

3 Before Disneyland

   a) Mike hadn't enjoyed any of his previous jobs.

   b) Mike had worked in many areas of engineering.

   c) Mike had specialised in one area of engineering.

4 He particularly likes the fact that

   a) he can concentrate by working on his own.

   b) there are fewer limits on him.

   c) he is in charge of a team.

5 Mike likes the fact that Big Thunder

   a) was originally designed in Japan.

   b) was his first ever project for Disney.

   c) received such a positive response from the public.

VOCABULARY: space

> ### LEARN BETTER: vocabulary
> Use a good dictionary like the Longman Active Study Dictionary to help you with new words and their definitions

3 Match these words to their definitions. Use a dictionary to help you.

devastation	meteorite	collision	comet
deflect	asteroid	threat	impact

1 A piece of rock that falls from space and lands on the Earth. _____

2 A rock the size of a small planet which travels around the sun. _____

3 To make something move in a different direction. _____

4 A bright object in space with a tail of gas and dust. _____

5 Damage or destruction to a large area or number of people. _____

6 The moment when one object hits another. _____

7 When a moving object hits something by accident. _____

8 A situation that could be dangerous. _____

GRAMMAR: the passive

4 There are five examples of the passive form in the article on page 61 'A rollercoaster of a job'. Underline them.

5 Rewrite each sentence in the passive form.

1 Rolls Royce employed Mike Kent.

Mike Kent _was employed by Rolls Royce._

2 We use a satellite in space for telecommunications.

A satellite in space _____
_____ .

3 My manager is always telling me not to do other people's jobs.

I am always _____
_____ .

4 Disneyland has created a new attraction.

A new attraction _____
_____ .

5 Visitors can enjoy Big Thunder at every Disneyland in the world.

Big Thunder _____
_____ .

6 We'll launch four more rockets this year.

Four more rockets _____
_____ .

7 Humans can't save the planet from a meteorite collision.

The planet _____
_____ .

8 The hurricane didn't hit our town.

Our town _____ .

6 Write the verb in brackets in the correct active <u>or</u> passive form in this article.

Halley's Comet is famous because it can easily
1 _____ _be seen_ _____ (see) from the earth. It
2 _____ (name) after the English astronomer, Edmond Halley (1656–1742). However, it
3 _____ (appear) many times over the centuries and often brings bad news.

Here are some facts about the comet:

- The Chinese first 4_____ (observe) it in 240 BC.

- 1066 AD Halley's Comet flew over England and the King 5 _____ (kill) in battle.

- 1910 The first photograph 6 _____ (take) of the comet.

- 1986 The NASA Space Shuttle Challenger 7 _____ (explode) only 73 seconds after it 8 _____ (launch) to meet the comet.

- Halley's Comet will 9 _____ (see) from the Earth again in 2061.

GRAMMAR: articles

1 Write the missing articles in this quiz. Write *the, a, an* or *0 (no article)*.

1 What type of animal is _the_ sloth?

a) _____ mammal   b) _____ fish

c) _____ insect

2 In which mountain range can you find _____ ancient Inca city?

a) _____ Andes   b) _____ Himalayas

c) _____ Alps

3 What is _____ capital of Germany?

a) _____ Bonn   b) _____ Munich

c) _____ Berlin

4 The 'Chunnel' is ____ tunnel which connects ___ France with

a) _____ Norway.   b) _____ England.

c) _____ Spain.

5 Where can you find ____ White House?

a) New York   b) Washington
c) Hollywood

6 What country is _____ Hong Kong in?

a) _____ Hong Kong   b) _____ China

c) _____ Great Britain

7 What is _____ world's longest river?

a) _____ Nile   b) _____ Amazon

c) _____ Mississippi

8 The Bullet in Japan is _____ type of

a) missile.   b) sushi.   c) train.

9 Where will you find _____ oysters?

a) under _____ sea   b) in trees   c) on land

10 The Three Gorges Dam is in

a) _____ United Arab Emirates.

b) _____ China.   c) _____ Caribbean.

2 Now try the quiz. How many can you score out of ten? Check your answers on page 93.

3 Decide if the use of articles is correct (3) or incorrect (7) in each sentence.

Example: That's ~~the~~ *a* nice coat. Is it new? ✗

1 Did you see the designs I told you about?

2 I went to the India last year.

3 The Caspian Sea is the largest enclosed body of water on Earth.

4 Weather hasn't been too good recently, has it?

5 Being in a Shakespeare play is a actor's dream.

6 It's one of the ugliest buildings in the city.

7 What's a width of this door?

8 We have a major problem with the new structure.

9 When does King make his speech?

10 Temperatures in the Dubai reach over 40°C.

EXTRA VOCABULARY: word building

4 Complete this table with the adjective and noun forms of these words.

adjectives	noun
high	height
wide	
	length
deep	
	square
	circle
triangular	

LEARN BETTER

When you learn a new word, think about how many other words you can create with it. Can you also use it as a verb, an adjective or a noun? Does it have prefixes and suffixes? Build new words in your notebook using a table like Exercise 4.

5 Complete these sentences with words from the table.

1 A: How _____ is the new tower going to be?

   B: About 1,000 metres, which will make it the tallest in the city.

2 Be careful children! That swimming pool is very _____ .

3 The office space in the building will be about 3,000 _____ metres in total.

4 Can you tell me what's the exact _____ of that cupboard? It might not fit between these two walls.

5 That _____ sign is a warning to slow down.

6 You start a football match with the ball in the centre _____ of the field.

LISTENING

6 [2.17] An engineer is presenting plans for a new tunnel under the sea. Listen and write the missing information including numbers and figures.

- New tunnel: a set of ^{1}_____ tubes.
- Length of tunnel = ^{2}_____ .
- That is about ^{3}_____ longer than the Channel Tunnel between ^{4}_____ .
- Length under the sea = ^{5}_____ .
- ^{6}_____ of the undersea section = 45 metres.
- Average journey time by train = ^{7}_____ .
- Typical speed of trains = ^{8}_____ .
- Overall cost (approx.) = ^{9}_____ .

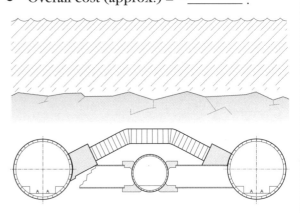

PRONUNCIATION

7a [2.18] Write each word next to the correct vowel sound.

depth	ski	wide	dish	shape	height
length	width	deep	eight	high	

/e/ _depth_ , _____

/ɪ/ _____ , _____

/iː/ _____ , _____

/aɪ/ _____ , _____ , _____

/eɪ/ _____ , _____

7b [2.18] Listen and check your answers. Now listen again and practise saying the words.

PRONOUNCE BETTER

Because many English words don't sound the same as they are written, it's a good idea to make a list of words with the same sound, as in Exercise 7.

LISTENING

1 [2.19] **Three university lecturers are discussing who to invite to talk to a group of design and engineering students. Listen and answer questions 1–5.**

1 What kind of building has Malcolm Bernier just finished?

a) A tower

b) A tunnel

c) A train

2 His buildings are considered by many to be…

a) interesting.

b) boring.

c) ugly.

3 What kind of event do they decide to have?

a) A talk

b) A presentation

c) A debate

4 What has been built by Lance Weiss?

a) A ski slope

b) A bridge

c) A tower

DICTATION

2 [2.19] **Listen again and write in the missing parts of the discussion.**

A: _____

Malcolm Bernier _____

_____ Randalf Tower?

B: Great idea. Do you think he'd be free?

A: _____

_____ .

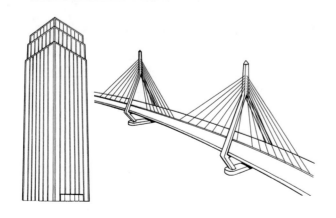

C: Sorry, but I don't think that's a good idea. His buildings are often criticised for being ugly.

A: Well, _____

_____ . The students will have lots of questions.

C: I don't know about that. And he isn't very good at talks. _____

_____ .

B: What about _____

_____

_____

_____ ?

A: That's a possible solution. What do you think about that?

C: Yes, _____

_____ .

A: We all agree then. We'll do that.

B: _____

Lance Weiss? He _____

_____ .

KEY LANGUAGE: discussing options, making decisions

3 **Find phrases in the discussion in Exercise 1 which mean the same as these.**

1 I'm not sure about that idea.

_____

2 How about …

_____

3 That's one possibility.

_____

4 Do you agree with that?

_____

5 Sounds good.

_____

6 I suggest we ask Lance Weiss.

_____

7 Let's do that then.

_____

STUDY SKILLS: preparing for a talk

1 Rachel is emailing advice to a friend who is going to give a talk. Underline the correct word.

Hi Emma
Great to hear from you again. Your talk sounds very exciting. I think the main thing is that your talk should ¹*reach/match* your audience's needs and interests. Try to structure it into ²*sections/messages* and think about the points you want to ³*make/do*. To help you remember, why don't you put your notes on ⁴*software/cards*? And don't forget to number them in the right order. Recently I saw a really good talk with visual ⁵*aids/helps* using PowerPoint. That's also a good way to help you speak in a logical order. I always find that if you have an introduction with some kind of ⁶*hook/bang* to get people's attention and then have a conclusion which makes ⁷*a collision/ an impact*, the rest just follows. So don't be nervous. You'll be fine!
Love
Rachel

WRITING: describing a process

2 Read this description of a new engineering idea for heating roads. Write in the missing words and expressions for sequencing the different stages from a–h.

POWER ON THE ROAD

There are now more and more ways to use the power of the sun as alternative energy. Henk Verweijmeren recently realised that ¹ _c)_ use the heat in roads. He took the original idea from looking at sheep warming themselves on a stretch of Scottish road. ² _____ he realised that roads could store and then convert the heat of the sun into more heat; ³ _____ , in the same way that a solar cell does. ⁴ _____ , pipes are put beneath the road. ⁵ _____ , cool water is pumped through the pipes ⁶ _____ the road is warmed by the sun. The road and surrounding soil and sand store the heat with 95 percent efficiency. ⁷ _____ is for the water to become warm. ⁸ _____ , the hot water in the pipes can be used to melt snow on roads, on airport runways or even fill your water heater.

a) From his observations   e) Finally

b) Next   f) for example

c) one way is to   g) The next stage

d) and then   h) First of all

3 Number these stages to produce and launch a new type of bicycle

_____ Build a prototype based on results.

_____ Invite journalists to the press launch.

_____ Do market research. Interview potential customers.

_____ Test the prototype.

_____ Make any modifications and test again.

4 Complete this paragraph describing the process in Exercise 3.

First of all *you need to do some market research*.
One way to do this is _____ .
Then, the next stage _____ and
_____ . From the results of that
_____ .
Finally, _____
_____ .

10.1 IT'S THE NEW THING

1 **Write the correct word in each space.**

| trendsetters charisma spread outbreak |
| influential imitate must-have |

Tom Ford has been one of the most ¹_____
fashion designers and ²_____ of the last twenty
years. He studied in New York but news of his talents
quickly ³_____ to Milan. In 1990 he moved to
Gucci where his ability to create ⁴_____ fashion
items, combined with his natural ⁵_____ , quickly
brought him fame and the post of design director.
Over the years many designers have tried to
⁶_____ the 'Ford look' but none have come close.
Now, working on his own, Ford is about to launch his
own line of products and with it will come another
⁷_____ of Ford madness.

2a 2.20 **Listen to these words. Where is the stress?
Categorise them in the table.**

| connectors imitate charisma cultural |
| economic influential community |
| trendsetters behaviour epidemics |

o o o	o O o	o O o o	o o O o
	connectors		

2b 2.20 **Listen again and practise saying the
words.**

VOCABULARY: phrasal verbs (3)

3 **Write in the missing particle.**

| over   down   out   with   on   out   into |
| on |

1 How long do you think it will be before this new
style catches _____ ?

2 Where did you find _____ about this new
trend?

3 Why do people buy _____ such awful fashions?

4 I can't keep up _____ all these changes.

5 Pink has taken _____ from orange this season.

6 The popularity of black clothes will never die

_____ .

7 I thought it would be popular but no one picked up
_____ the idea.

8 I think the interest in violent films has slowed

_____ .

TRANSLATION

4 **Translate these sentences with phrasal verbs into
your language.**

1 It'll never catch on.

_____

2 Long hair for men died out in the eighties.

_____

3 I don't buy into that idea.

_____

4 We like to keep up with the latest trends.

_____

5 Did the boss pick up on your idea?

_____

6 Trends usually slow down after a short time.

_____

READING

1 Read the article and correct these statements.

1 Fashions and trends change at ~~different speeds~~ *a steady rate* according to the research.

2 We think that a few of our decisions about fashion are made independently.

3 Few celebrities influence us and are copied by us.

4 The speed at which Americans buy albums changes a lot.

5 None of the things tested for their popularity changed at a steady rate.

2 Complete this summary of the article about changes in fashion. Use words from the article.

New research shows that [1]_____ often change, but this [2]_____ is at a constant rate. This shows that most of us [3]_____ others when it comes to fashion. The people we follow are called [4]_____ and we are interested in celebrities who often change their ideas. Similarly, our taste in music may change but this change is at a constant [5]_____ . The same is also true for [6]_____ and [7]_____ .

FASHIONS CHANGE, BUT CHANGE IS ALWAYS THE FASHION

Fashions change at a steady rate, new research suggests. They are driven by a minority of innovators with many people copying each other. These are the conclusions of university researchers from the UK and USA.

The research also challenges the belief that a lot of our fashion choices are independent, rational decisions. It shows we generally copy others when it comes to popular culture.

The researchers say innovation is what actually drives fashion change. 'Innovators are the cool ones who "pump" new fashions into our world,' Dr Bentley of Durham University explains. 'Most are ignored, but some get copied.'

Plenty of celebrities, for example, get copied. Dr Bentley also points out that we are not necessarily looking out for the latest fashion but we need regular change.

Similar results to those of Dr Bentley were found in the US when academics looked at the Billboard Top 200 chart and found that it turned over at a constant average rate for 30 years, from the 1950s to the 1980s. The number of albums entering and exiting the chart varied from day to day and month to month, but overall the average change was 5.6 percent per month for the full 30-year period. They discovered similar consistency in the fashions for baby names and dog breeds.

They looked at the popularity of music, baby names and types of dogs and found that their popularity changes at a steady rate, regardless of population size.

VOCABULARY: adjective order

3 Write one of these adjectives in the right position in each sentence.

| red wedding digital wooden ~~garden~~ |
| leather dinner blue |

1 A plastic ∧ *garden* chair.

2 Andy Warhol wore a black jacket.

3 She looked wonderful in her white dress.

4 James Bond often wears a black jacket.

5 Put it in this picture frame.

6 I usually just wear a pair of ordinary jeans.

7 There's a pretty blouse in the window.

8 It's a silver watch.

LISTENING

4 [2.21] Listen to five speakers talking about the objects below. Write the object a–f next to the speaker. There is one extra object.

Speaker 1: ___   Speaker 4: ___

Speaker 2: ___   Speaker 5: ___

Speaker 3: ___

a)

b)

c)

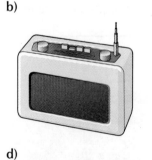

d)

e)

f)

GRAMMAR: expressions of quantity

5 Choose the correct answer, a, b or c.

1 We work with ___ designers from Rome.

a) a little   b) a few   c) little

2 I gave them ___ ideas to help them.

a) a couple of   b) a lot   c) plenty

3 There are ___ people asking for this kind of haircut.

a) a lot   b) plenty   c) a lot of

4 ___ of students in my class are from abroad.

a) Plenty   b) Enough   c) None

5 ___ people aren't interested in fashion at all.

a) None   b) A couple   c) Many

6 There are ___ celebrities who have a lot of influence over our tastes.

a) some   b) plenty   c) a lot

7 Do you have ___ money to buy this?

a) enough   b) many   c) a few

8 I have ___ time for looking at new fashions and knowing what's popular.

a) little   b) a couple of   c) few

6 Choose the correct quantifier for each sentence.

| plenty none of couple enough a few |
| some |

1 Can you spare me _____ minutes? I have a question.

2 _____ my friends works here.

3 We don't have _____ money for this.

4 There's _____ of milk in the fridge if you'd like some.

5 _____ people have a unique fashion but most follow what they see on TV.

6 Only a _____ of friends came to my birthday party. It was a small event!

LISTENING

1a Answer these questions

1 Which race on earth has always wanted to live longer?

_____

2 Which do you think live longer, men or women?

_____

3 How could people live longer?

_____

4 Why don't some people want to live longer?

_____

1b 2.22 Now listen and check your answers

2a Decide if these sentences true or false according to the interview.

1 It's important for humans to live on their own in order to live longer. _____

2 One reason we are living longer is because of improvements in medicine. _____

3 Estimates show that one person in 100,000 is aged 100 or above. _____

4 Science can prove why women live longer than men. _____

5 People over 100 tend to have a positive and relaxed attitude to life. _____

6 Only the richest members of society live a long time. _____

7 Our genes have some control over how long we will live. _____

8 The doctor doesn't think it's always a good idea to live to 100. _____

2b 2.22 Listen again and check your answers.

DICTATION

3 2.22 Read these sentences taken from Doctor Stivers' replies. Listen again and complete each sentence.

1 Yes, it's true that the human race has always

_____

_____ for so long.

2 …living longer also means we _____

_____ .

3 As humans we work towards medical advances and

_____

_____ helps.

4 We estimate that there is currently _____

_____

_____ .

5 In fact, in recent years, the average lifespan for men

_____

_____ .

6 Eat well, so … lots of fruit and vegetables. Few overweight people live to be a hundred and

_____

_____ a hundred.

7 People who are a hundred are good at _____

_____ and also

tend not to be poor.

8 I think people who worry about living longer are in danger of _____ .

And just because you live to 101, it _____

_____ .

PRONUNCIATION

4a `2.23` **Listen to eight sentences and tick the number you hear.**

1	13	30
2	14 percent	40 percent
3	2008	2080
4	1950	1915
5	100	900
6	51.3	50.13
7	110,000	10,000
8	100,000,000	1,000,000

4b `2.23` **Listen again and practise saying the sentences.**

GRAMMAR: infinitives and *-ing* forms

5 **Underline the correct form. If both forms are possible, then underline both.**

1 Will good food enable people *to live/living* longer?

2 I don't want *to work/working* when I'm 65.

3 We don't need to keep on *to travel/travelling* tonight.

4 Do you enjoy *to shop/shopping* for new fashions?

5 At what age did you start *to worry/worrying* about money.

6 They promised *to pick/picking* us up from the airport.

7 He succeeded in *to convince/convincing* them to employ him.

8 I like *to walk/walking* early in the morning.

9 We managed *to change/changing* the course we're doing.

10 She decided *to buy/buying* completely new clothes for the summer.

11 They don't expect anyone *to turn up/turning up* for the party.

12 Do you allow anyone *to join/joining* the library?

13 Would you like *to have/having* something to eat?

14 Many people hate *to learn/learning* something new or complicated.

15 Romeo and Juliet continued *to see/seeing* each other even after their parents tried *to stop/stopping* them.

6 **Write the verbs in brackets in the infinitive or *-ing* form.**

Rose Pervis celebrates her hundredth birthday tomorrow. She says the secret to her long life is because she believes in ¹_____ (eat) fresh vegetables and ²_____ (have) a cup of green tea before bed. Rose said: 'The other secret to long life is that I've always loved ³_____ (walk) in my garden every morning. I know some people do lots of exercise but I've never been interested in ⁴_____ (run) or things like that.'

People in the town of Willington where Rose lives are hoping ⁵_____ (celebrate) her long life with a party. 'We'd like ⁶_____ (show) Rose how important she is to us,' said local town councillor, Lorna Rodgers. 'Everyone in the town has been involved in ⁷_____ (organise) this special event. We decided ⁸_____ (use) it as an opportunity to bring together everyone in the town as well as giving her our best wishes.' Rose says she's grateful to everyone for ⁹_____ (arrange) the party and she's also looking forward to ¹⁰_____ (have) another one for her hundred and first birthday next year.

KEY LANGUAGE:
the language of meetings

1 Here is a discussion at a meeting. Replace each phrase in bold, a–g, with one of the phrases, 1–7.

1 Please make your ___

2 your comment. ___

3 it isn't acceptable ___

4 We're here ___

5 unhappy ___

6 just say something please? ___

7 the matter ___

A: Good morning everyone. (a) **The purpose of this meeting is** to discuss the facilities for older people at the beach. Who would like to begin?

B: I would. I'm very (b) **concerned** that we have to pay to get to the beach. It doesn't help that the car park is a fifteen-minute walk from the beach…

A: (c) **Go ahead with your** main point.

B: Well, (d) **I'm afraid I can't agree** that we should pay. It should be free for pensioners to get on to the beach.

A: I see how you feel. Thank you for (e) **that**. I'll look into (f) **it.**

C: Sorry, can I (g) **make a comment?**

A: Sure. Go ahead.

2 `2.24` Listen and check your answers.

STUDY SKILLS:
recording and learning vocabulary

1 Study this page from a Spanish learner's notebook. Tick the study techniques in the checklist that the learner uses.

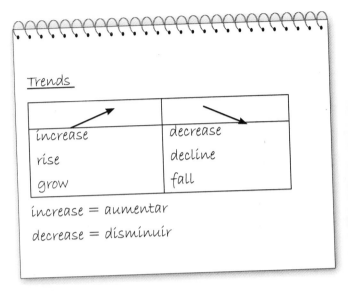

Trends

increase ↗	decrease ↘
rise	decline
grow	fall

increase = aumentar

decrease = disminuir

o O
de<u>crease</u> (v)

O o
<u>de</u>crease (n)

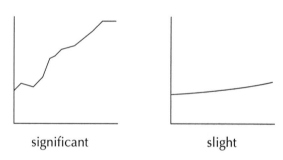

significant   slight

There has been a significant improvement in my English this term.

My salary at work has remained stable for two years.

translation of words   ☑

write definition   ☐

word stress   ☐

parts of speech   ☐

write collocations   ☐

categorise words   ☐

write a useful sentence with new words in   ☐

draw diagram or picture   ☐

2 Choose some more trend words from page 111 of the course book. Design your own page to help you learn these words.

WRITING SKILLS:
describe a trend

3 Match descriptions a–f to the six graphs and charts.

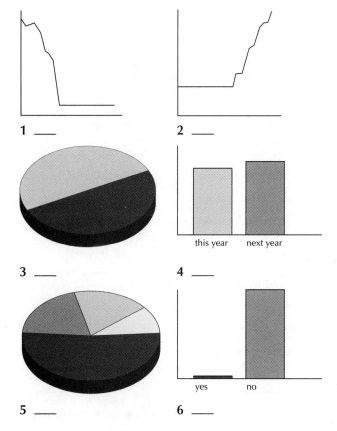

1 ___   2 ___

3 ___   4 ___

this year   next year

5 ___   6 ___

yes   no

a) This pie chart shows the results of a study carried out on school children. The figures compare how they spend their free time, with over half now playing computer games.

b) The level of spending on Asia and Africa is constant, with both sectors receiving about the same.

c) The findings on this chart show that the overall number of positive and negative answers from the group was significantly different.

d) We concluded that the sudden rise and overall improvement was due to the large investment and attention to spending that took place in the previous year.

e) Earlier in the year there was a marked fall and then sales remained relatively stable for the remaining six months.

f) We predict that next year's figure will go up by about 10 percent on current forecasts.

4 Write full sentences with trend words to answer these questions.

1 What is the current rate of inflation in your country?

The rate was steady last year but it's currently

increasing by about two percent a year.

_____

_____

2 How would you describe the change in unemployment figures in your country over the last ten years?

_____

_____

_____

_____

3 How would you describe your progress in English in the last few months. (Include any marks from tests you have done.)

_____

_____

_____

_____

4 How would you describe the changes in house prices in your country over the last five years?

_____

_____

_____

_____

11 Arts and media

11.1 TYPES OF MEDIA

1 Match each genre to a picture.

Soul Horror Crime Autobiography Animation ~~Reggae~~ Science Fiction Jazz Opera Classical

1 ___Reggae___

2 _____

3 _____

4 _____

5 _____

6 _____

7 _____

8 _____

9 _____

My Life Bill Clinton

10 _____

2 Each speaker is talking about something from a book, TV show or film. Match one of these words to each description.

character series plot atmosphere chapter novel

1 The film begins in a scary house and it's really dark.

_____

2 It's so complicated that after fifteen minutes you don't know who is who and what is happening.

_____

3 I've just got one more to read. _____

4 This is his best yet. I've read all the others but this is great fiction! _____

5 Last week they found out it was his son. What happened this week? I missed it I'm afraid.

_____

6 I really like her. She's evil but the most interesting person in it. _____

3 Underline the correct adjective.

1 It's such a *moving/outstanding* piece of music. I cry every time I hear it.

2 It's *hilarious/breathtaking*! It must be the funniest show on TV.

3 The actor gave *an outstanding/a classic* performance. It was perhaps the only time we'll ever see that play performed so well.

4 This *groundbreaking/incomparable* technology allows them to film deep beneath the oceans.

4 2.25 Listen and match each word with the correct stress pattern.

affairs	O o	_____
country	o O	___affairs___
entertainment	O o o	_____
computer	o O o	_____
groundbreaking	o o O o	_____
incomparable	o O o o o	_____

READING

1 Read the text about Greta Garbo and decide if the statements are true or false.

It has been said that she was the most beautiful woman who ever lived. Whether this is true or not, Greta Garbo will always be remembered for starring in some of Hollywood's greatest masterpieces, from the silent movies of the twenties through to her last film in 1941. Her decision never to make a film again shocked the movie world. She accepted an honorary Oscar in 1954 but soon afterwards she was rarely seen in public again. She famously said, 'I want to be alone.' She bought a seven-room apartment in New York City where she lived on her own for the rest of her life. Throughout the years leading up to her death in 1990, Garbo wasn't a total recluse. It was reported that she still spent time with the rich and famous and that she would go for long walks in New York wearing dark glasses and casual clothes. She had invested the money she had made from films wisely and there are still rumours that she wrote an autobiography. However, the book has never been published. Her final interview took place in Cannes with the journalist Paul Callan. He started the interview by saying, 'I wonder…' Garbo interrupted, said, 'Why wonder?' and walked away. It is probably one of the shortest interviews in celebrity history.

1 She made films during three decades. ____

2 All her films were silent. ____

3 People were surprised when she ended her career in 1941. ____

4 She lived in New York until she died. ____

5 She never saw anyone ever again after 1954. ____

6 After she stopped making films, she could afford not to work. ____

7 You can read her autobiography. ____

8 In her final interview, Garbo let the journalist finish his first question. ____

VOCABULARY: words connected with the arts

2 Match the best word in the left column with each category on the right.

1 bestseller   a) music

2 blockbuster   b) work of art

3 critic   c) payment

4 royalty   d) person

5 household name   e) film

6 hit   f) celebrity

7 masterpiece   g) book

3 Complete these sentences with words from the left column in Exercise 2.

1 One _____ said that he had fallen asleep during it but I really enjoyed it.

2 She earned a 15 percent _____ every time the book was sold.

3 It's too early to say if that painting will become a

_____ .

4 He's still a _____ even though he's been a recluse for the last ten years.

5 It became a _____ and stayed at number one in the charts for ten weeks.

6 Harry Potter is the biggest children's

_____ this century.

7 The trouble with all these _____ movies is that they have lots of special effects and little real acting.

GRAMMAR: reported speech

4 Read each pair of sentences, direct and reported speech. Underline the correct words to make the second sentence reported speech.

1 'I run a lot.'

He told me that *I run/he ran* a lot.

2 'Lisa can't talk today.'

She said Lisa *didn't/couldn't* talk *this day/that day*.

3 'Please go.'

He asked me *went/to go*.

4 'Leonardo is going to get married.'

I heard last week that Leonardo *went/was going* to get married.

5 'I've been here before.'

He said she *have/had* been *there/then* before.

6 'We'll work on it again tomorrow.'

They agreed they *worked/would work* on it again *that day/the next* day.

7 'Sam is writing her autobiography.'

Last year Sam *was writing/had written* her autobiography.

8 'Turn left.'

The policeman *said/told* me *to turn/turn* left.

9 'You are the best in the class this year.'

My teacher told me I *have been/was* the best in the class *that/next* year.

10 'You've done badly on this test Sally.'

The teacher told *she/her* that she *had been doing/had done* badly on the test.

5 Complete each sentence as reported speech.

1 'It was a terrible performance.'

The critics said it _____ a terrible performance.

2 'I want to end the interview at this point.'

The actress said she _____ to end the interview at that point.

3 'You'll never be famous.'

His father said he _____ famous.

4 'Download a copy of their new CD.'

She told me _____ a copy of their new CD.

5 'The children are enjoying the DVD.'

She said they _____ the DVD.

6 'I'd like you to star in my next film.'

The director said he _____ her _____ in his next film.

6 Report the following sentences.

1 'She's working as a model to support her family.'

The reporter said _____

2 'I think it's ours.'

My brother said _____

3 'We'll visit you sometime.'

Her grand children said _____

4 'They worked on this project for three months.'

Rashid said _____

5 ''I can't go to the theatre tonight.'

My sister said _____

7 Read this script from an interview with a famous actress. Then complete the article reporting what she said.

'I didn't like working with my first film company which was the reason I moved. Then I met my first husband and it was a very romantic time. When he died I was devastated. I thought to myself, 'I can't work again.' So I sold our house and have been living on my boat in the Mediterranean ever since. I haven't been a recluse but I didn't want to meet journalists. Then one day this film script was sent to me. I loved the script and so I've decided to start work again.'

The actress said that she *hadn't liked working* with her first film company which *had been* the reason why she _____ . Then she _____ first husband and it _____ a very romantic time. When he _____ devastated. She _____ to herself that she _____ again.
So she _____ house and _____ boat in the Mediterranean ever since that time. She _____ a recluse but she _____ to meet journalists. Then one day _____ film script _____ . She _____ the script and so she _____ to start work again.

LISTENING

1a An interviewer (I) is speaking to Marlene (M), a fashion model and TV star. Match his questions a–g to the answers 1–6. There is one extra question.

a) Do you get tired of the cameras?

b) Didn't you enjoy it?

c) Does that bother you?

d) Do you like being a celebrity?

e) Does that mean you are having a break from fashion modelling as well?

f) So has the TV show changed your life?

g) Do you think you'll do another?

I: Hello, Marlene. You've just finished your first TV show. ¹ _____ ?

M: I'll take some time off first.

I: Why's that? ² _____ ?

M: No. I loved doing the show…

I: ³ _____ ?

M: No. In fact I'm going to Milan for a clothes photo shoot next week.

I: I see. ⁴ _____ ?

M: No, it hasn't, though more people recognise me …

I: ⁵ _____ ?

M: Yes it does, a bit. I used to be able to go the supermarket but …

I: ⁶ _____ ?

M: No, never, I've been doing this kind of thing for five years…

1b 2.26 Listen and check your answers.

DICTATION

2 2.26 Listen again and write in the missing parts of Marlene's answers.

M: No. I loved doing the show _____

_____ .

M: No, it hasn't, though more people recognise me

_____

_____

_____ .

M: Yes, it does, a bit. I used to be able to go to the supermarket but _____

_____

_____

_____ .

M: No, never. I've been doing this kind of thing for five years. _____

_____

_____

_____ .

GRAMMAR: reported questions

3 Read the interviewer's questions as reported questions. Correct the mistakes in 1–6.

1 'Do you think you'll do another TV show?'

   would do
   The journalist asked me if I thought I ~~had done~~ another TV show.

2 'Why don't you want to do any more TV?'

   The journalist asked me to I not want to do any more TV.

3 'Are you leaving modelling?'

   The journalist asked me if I had been leaving modelling.

4 'How much time do you spend travelling?'

   The journalist asked me if I spent how much time travelling.

5 'How long have you been a model?'

   The journalist asked me how long I would be a model.

6 'Do you get tired of the cameras?'

   The journalist asked me what I did get tired of the cameras.

READING

4 Read this careers article about being a foreign correspondent. Write these words and phrases in the correct places.

chutzpah	wangle	far and wide	integrity
convey	home	undaunted	cover

5 Read the article again and complete sentences 1–5.

1 Some journalists want to become a foreign correspondent because

a) the life is exciting.

b) the life is tough.

c) they can go to different places.

2 To get a job as a foreign correspondent, you must be

a) sensitive.

b) determined.

c) sociable.

3 An editor will be most impressed with you if you

a) have lots of skills.

b) have already travelled round the world.

c) can speak another language.

4 You may be able to get sent as a correspondent if you are

a) clever and maybe even a little dishonest.

b) apply in writing.

c) work on a local newspaper.

5 Newspaper editors will send journalists who

a) regularly call the editor and report back.

b) like to ask questions and listen to orders.

c) have enough courage to do something, even against authority.

6 Which advice best sums up the final paragraph?

a) Find out the correct information.

b) Give readers a real sense of the events.

c) Have high moral standards

CAREERS IN JOURNALISM: BECOMING A FOREIGN CORRESPONDENT

So, you want to be a foreign correspondent. Unfortunately so do lots of other journalists. Many see it as their free passport to travel 1_____ . As the world gets smaller, the competition for working overseas gets tougher. But if you remain 2_____ you could be able to 3_____ your way into reporting on the latest crisis.

Some journalists say that they want to be foreign correspondents 'while they can'. After a few years of work, they reason, they can settle down to a comfortable job and 4_____ less adventurous stories at home. But whenever you decide to go, here are some skills and talents you'll need:

LEARN A FOREIGN LANGUAGE

Many correspondents find that they need to work among several languages, but knowing at least one very well will increase your skills and show editors that you have an aptitude for language.

INDEPENDENCE AND 5_____

No newspaper editor will send a reporter who needs a lot of direction and management while reporting to their boss half a world away. You'll need plenty of self-confidence and be prepared sometimes to break some rules.

BE THE BEST

Many journalists can report well but foreign correspondents also need to be great writers. You have to be able to 6_____ the scene of war to readers in less than 1000 wo – with bombs and bullets going off around you. Every word you write need to bring 7_____ readers what's really happening wi objective honesty and 8_____ .

KEY LANGUAGE:
comparing and contrasting

1 `2.27` Listen to a man and woman comparing some DVDs. Number the DVDs (1–4) in the order which they are discussed. Which DVD isn't discussed?

☐

☐

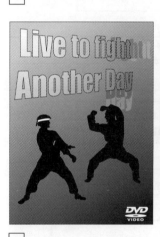

☐

☐

☐

2a Complete the conversation with these missing phrases. There is one extra phrase.

much better	less serious	very different
worse than	same as	very similar

M: So, what do you fancy this evening?

W: Nothing violent. I don't want you to get any more of those films with endless fight scenes and awful acting.

M: How about this one?

W: But that's by the same director.

M: Yes, but it's ¹_____ from his others.

W: Well, the front looks ²_____ with all those people fighting. How about a nice romantic comedy? I haven't seen this one before.

M: We must be able to find something ³_____ than that. It'll just be lots of kissing in fields. What's this?

W: It's that TV series about global warming. It's beautifully filmed, but I'd rather watch something ⁴_____ this evening.

M: This looks good. It's set on a spaceship and slowly everyone disappears.

W: I suppose we could do a lot ⁵_____ that. I do like the actress in it.

2b `2.27` Listen and check your answers.

EXTRA VOCABULARY:
talking about films

3 Write each word and phrase in the correct place in the table.

complex	stunning special effects	thriller
action	many locations around the world	
good versus evil	romantic comedy	
twists and turns	science fiction	
superbly choreographed fight scenes		

Genre	Plot	Special features
	complex	

STUDY SKILLS: delivering a talk

1 `2.28` Listen to a student talking at the beginning of a meeting. Tick (✔) the things he does on the checklist.

How to give an effective talk:

- Explain the purpose of your talk. ✔

- Speak clearly in a loud voice.

- Structure your talk with words like *Firstly, Secondly, Finally…*

- Involve your audience by asking them a question.

- Tell your audience when they can ask questions.

- Start with a joke or funny story.

SPEAK BETTER

When you are going to give a talk in English, here are some useful ways to prepare beforehand:

- record and listen to yourself.
- practise on a friend.
- practise in front of the mirror.

WRITING SKILLS: a report

2 Write the missing words to complete these sentences from a report.

| majority   overall   general   almost |
| whole   most |

1 _____ , we had a large number of people at the open day.

2 _____ of the people were students from the university.

3 _____ all of them stayed for two hours.

4 The _____ gave positive feedback on the event.

5 On the _____ everything went according to plan.

6 In _____ the committee feels it could be organised in the same way next year.

3 Study each piece of information about audiences at a street festival. Complete the sentence to summarise the information. See the example.

Age range of audience:	
Children:	9%
18–45 year olds:	85%
Over 45:	6%

1 *On the whole,* _____

_____

_____

People came to the festival:	
with family:	73%
with friends:	20%
on their own:	7%

2 *The majority* _____

_____

_____

Audience feedback on the performers at the event:	
Excellent:	91%
Good:	8%
Poor:	1%

3 *Almost all* _____

_____

_____

Audience feedback on food and refreshments:	
Satisfied:	13%
Not satisfied:	75%
No opinion:	12%

4 *In general* _____

_____

_____

12.1 REAL CRIMES?

VOCABULARY: words from the lesson

1 Read this letter in response to the newspaper report on page 123 of the coursebook. Complete the letter with words from 1–10, a, b, or c.

Dear Sir

I read with interest your story yesterday about the young cyber ¹_____. My view of the ²_____ is that the boy in question should be put into some kind of prison for ³_____. We cannot continue to have these types of individuals ⁴_____ the net and being allowed to steal. By ignoring the ⁵_____ and not locking away such ⁶_____, judges are sending out the wrong message to young people. They are encouraging ⁷_____ card theft. Not only that, but we're paying taxes for our police force to ⁸_____ these crimes. If he was ⁹_____ with theft then obviously he should be punished and I think you will find that the ¹⁰_____ of sensible people feel the same way.

Dr R. Smithers, London.

EXTRA VOCABULARY: types of crime

2 What type of crime do the newspaper headlines refer to? Choose one of these crimes for 1–10.

arson	murder	blackmail	forgery
mugging	speeding	kidnapping	burglary
hacking	identify theft		

1 Employee sets fire to factory! *arson*

2 Jewellery taken from house while couple slept!
_____

3 Seventy-year-old with monthly pension attacked in street! _____

4 Boy uses neighbour's password to do online shopping! _____

5 False bank notes found in back of van!
_____

6 Police stop 200 kph driver! _____

7 Wife's body found in garden! _____

8 Million pounds asked for safe return of child!
_____

9 Company president pays thousands for return of embarrassing photos! _____

10 Teenager steals government information online!
_____

TRANSLATION

3 Translate the ten types of crime in Exercise 2 into your language.

1 _____		6 _____	
2 _____		7 _____	
3 _____		8 _____	
4 _____		9 _____	
5 _____		10 _____	

1 a) criminal   b) robber   c) robot

2 a) computer   b) case   c) police

3 a) someone   b) juveniles   c) people

4 a) surfing   b) emailing   c) texting

5 a) evidence   b) boy   c) news

6 a) keys   b) crimes   c) offenders

7 a) post   b) credit   c) PIN number

8 a) look up   b) find   c) investigate

9 a) caught   b) done   c) charged

10 a) majority   b) minority   c) most

THE CAUSES OF CRIME

VOCABULARY: word combinations

1 **Choose a word to complete each sentence. You can use some words more than once.**

behaviour tradition relationship link
decision circle

1 His prison sentence was reduced for good _____ .

2 Many people say crime is part of a vicious _____ caused by poverty.

3 I don't want to make a long-term career _____ until I've finished my degree.

4 I know a lot of people but only a few are part of my close _____ of friends.

5 Do you think there is a genetic _____ between personality and crime?

6 She has a very close _____ with her mother.

7 There's a long _____ in our family of all our relatives meeting in May for an annual reunion.

8 Most criminal _____ can be explained by a person's family background.

GRAMMAR: third conditional

2 **Underline the correct verb form.**

1 If I'd seen the man, I *would have stopped*/*would stop* him from stealing the car.

2 If the burglar had entered through the door and not the window, he *had set off*/*would have set off* the alarm.

3 If the same crime *had happened*/*happened* in my country, they would have got five years in prison.

4 If the police *have arrived*/*had arrived* ten minutes earlier, they would have captured the bank robbers.

5 She might have avoided a life of crime, if she *hadn't had*/*wouldn't have had* such a difficult childhood.

6 Other people *might do*/*might have done* something about the attack if they'd known the attacker didn't have a gun.

7 What *would you have said*/*would you say* if you'd met the burglar in your house?

8 They *wouldn't have let*/*wouldn't let* him go, if he hadn't been related to someone important.

3 **Write the verb in brackets in the correct form.**

1 I wouldn't have let my children watch TV, if I _____ (think) they were going to behave badly as a result.

2 If my uncle _____ (not/chose) a life of crime, he wouldn't have been happy.

3 What if you _____ (lock) the front door? Would that have stopped them?

4 If the detective had seen the clue, the police _____ (might/catch) them sooner.

5 You wouldn't have been a victim of identity theft if you _____ (keep) your password secret.

6 If I'd known she was the criminal, I _____ (never/invite) her to my house!

PRONUNCIATION: contracted forms

4 **2.29** **Listen to and repeat these third conditionals spoken at normal speed.**

1 I would have had breakfast if I had had time.

2 He might have gone to the party if he had known about it.

3 You wouldn't have been happy if you had married her.

4 Would they have caught the train if the taxi had come on time?

5 **2.30** **Now listen to and write eight sentences spoken at normal speed.**

1 _____

2 _____

3 _____

4 _____

5 _____

6 _____

7 _____

8 _____

6 Look at each set of three sentences. Match the halves of each sentence. Look back at the grammar sections on conditionals in units 4, 5 and 12 in the coursebook to help you.

1 If I'd known your number ___c)___

If I knew your number ___a)___

If you leave a message ___b)___

a) I'd call you.

b) I'll call you back.

c) I would have called you.

2 We'll see you later ____

We'd see you later ____

We'd have seen you last night ____

a) if you go there.

b) if you'd been there.

c) if you were coming.

3 If I had seen them ____

If I were you ____

If I see them ____

a) I would tell them.

b) I would have told them.

c) I'll tell them.

4 If my brother goes to a different university ____

If my brother had gone to a different university ____

If my brother went to a different university ____

a) he might have done better.

b) he'd do better.

c) he won't do as well.

5 We would have been on time ____

We'll leave on time ____

We'd be on time ____

a) if the taxi arrives now!

b) if we'd left earlier.

c) if it wasn't for the terrible traffic.

7 Read each situation and write a conditional sentence. See the first example.

Situation 1: Your friend wants advice about accepting a new job. You think it's a good job.

If _I were you, I'd take it._

Situation 2: You lent a friend $300. You wish you hadn't. You can't afford to go on holiday now.

If _____

Situation 3: A customer wants to buy a car. You can offer him a 20% discount today only.

If _____

Situation 4: Your friend can't make his new DVD work. Explain that you press the green button to make it switch on.

If _____

Situation 5: You wanted to take someone to a party last night. You didn't ask her/him.

If _____

Situation 6: The bus leaves in 10 minutes. Your friend needs to catch it. You can run from your house to the bus stop in 8 minutes.

If _____

Situation 7: You didn't study music at university. You always wanted to be a composer. You became an accountant.

If _____

Situation 8: You answered your mobile phone while driving. You crashed the car into a tree.

If _____

LISTENING

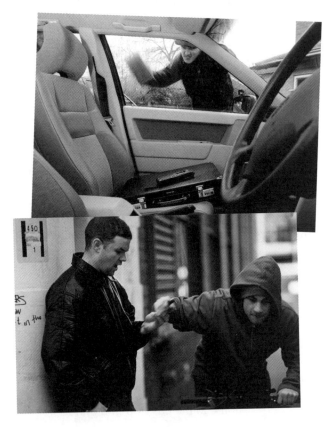

1 `2.31` **Listen to a news report. Tick which people are mentioned or referred to?**

The police

A prosecutor

A lawyer

A witness

A bank robber

A kidnapper

READING

2 **Read this extract from an article about crime in the world. Write the missing sub-headings (a–e) in the correct places in the text.**

a) Better protected from burglary

b) Car theft

c) The world is a safer place

d) Less robbery on the streets

e) An overall downward trend

NEW STATISTICS ON CRIME!

1 _____

New statistics show that, internationally, crime rates have fallen and so researchers have drawn the conclusion that more people than ever before can feel free to walk around without fear of crime.

2 _____

Take the USA, for example. It still ranks high in violent crime among industrialised nations but, on the whole, street crime here is at one of its lowest rates ever. Interestingly, there are some exceptions where crime has risen, but only a little: low-crime societies like Denmark and Finland have recently experienced small increases in street crime.

3 _____

Of course, comparing crime figures around the world is rather complicated. Each country has different definitions of what makes a crimes but if we look at the past two decades, for example, most countries suggest there has been an overall fall in the number of cases of goods being taken from individuals. In particular, many Asian and Arab World countries have brought much of this crime under greater control.

4 _____

For a long time this has been regarded as one of the worst types of property crimes but it is generally thought to be lower now than in the eighties. This could be due to more private homes and offices having better security systems from people breaking in. Some of the countries with the worst records are Australia, Canada, Denmark, England, Finland and Wales, while Korea, Saudi Arabia and Spain perform well.

5 _____

No surprises here. The country with the most vehicles per person is also the place with the highest recorded figures. After the USA, with over one million thefts per year, comes the UK, Japan and France.

VOCABULARY: people in crime

3 Read clues 1–12 and find the words in the word search below.

1 A criminal who steals.

2 Detectives look for these on windows.

3 Money for the return of a kidnap victim.

4 A victim held by criminals.

5 A person who represents people in court.

6 Police think this person might have done it.

7 Robbers make this when they escape.

8 People who take victims and ask for ransom.

9 They hold a lot of money.

10 What the person in number 1 is guilty of.

11 People who chase criminals.

12 A person who enters computer systems illegally.

T	H	I	E	F	S	H	A	C	K	E	R
H	O	R	R	I	B	D	C	B	A	N	F
I	N	G	E	N	P	O	L	A	A	L	K
E	S	T	E	G	E	T	A	N	K	A	I
S	U	S	P	E	C	T	E	K	O	W	D
G	S	P	E	R	L	A	W	S	E	Y	N
E	P	O	L	P	R	F	I	N	G	E	A
T	H	L	A	R	A	N	S	O	M	R	P
A	Z	I	C	I	N	I	N	A	L	Q	P
W	O	C	I	N	S	T	H	E	F	T	E
A	W	E	M	T	O	R	N	E	Y	E	R
Y	S	H	O	S	T	A	G	E	G	E	S

GRAMMAR: modal perfects

4 Match the first sentence, 1–4, to the correct second sentence, a–d.

1 They were the only people at the scene of the crime. ____

2 They didn't have the money. ____

3 I did see them spending a lot of money last night but maybe it was their own money. ____

4 They got ten years for taking the money. ____

a) They might have done it.

b) They must have done it.

c) They can't have done it.

d) They shouldn't have done it.

5 Underline the correct modal verb.

1 He didn't let me know it was happening. He *must/ should* have done!

2 I'm not sure if he wanted to come too. He *might/ must* have done but I didn't see him to tell him.

3 You *shouldn't/can't* have done that. It was a very bad thing to do.

4 The burglar *could/must* have got in from the back of the house. There's no other way in.

5 He *couldn't/shouldn't* have murdered her. He was with me when it happened.

6 Rewrite the first sentence with the words in the second sentence. Use a modal perfect.

1 There was glass on the floor.

The burglar *must have* broken the window.

2 The password had been written on a piece of paper.

The criminal _____ copied it from the owner.

3 He hasn't been at his desk. I'm certain he's been out all day.

He _____ in today.

4 It's possible that they took a getaway car.

They _____ a getaway car.

5 The victim screamed and shouted for help.

The victim _____ really scared.

6 The police didn't get here on time. The criminals got away.

The police _____ here earlier.

LISTENING

LISTEN BETTER

When you listen and make notes, try to predict some of the words before you listen.

1 **2.32** **Listen to a judge summing up a case for the jury. Number these pictures 1 to 4 in the order she mentions them.**

2a **A member of the jury is taking notes on the case. Read the notes and try to predict what types of words might be missing.**

> The accused went into the ¹_____ at 9p.m. on the ²_____ evening.
>
> He pulled out a ³_____ and told the cashier to ⁴_____ .
>
> The police caught him half an hour later with ⁵_____ in his car.
>
> We must decide either that:
>
> One: Kane is a dangerous ⁶_____ who should have been taken off our streets months ago.
>
> Two: Kane is a victim of his childhood because he never had any close ⁷_____ and so behaved badly at ⁸_____ .

2b **2.32** **Listen and check your answers**

KEY LANGUAGE: discussing court cases

3 **Write one of these words to complete each sentence.**

> witnesses   mind   evidence   innocent
> facts   defendant   punishment   jury
> minds   case

1 Let me summarise the main __facts__ for you.

2 The _____ clearly shows he is guilty.

3 I don't think the facts of the _____ are very clear.

4 I've made up my _____ .

5 There should be no doubt in your _____ that this man is guilty.

6 I will bring _____ who can confirm that the accused was there at the time of the kidnapping.

7 Members of the _____ , the facts are very simple.

8 I am confident that you will find the _____ guilty.

9 You have to decide the _____ to fit the crime.

10 I believe he's _____ because he has no other previous criminal record.

4 **Complete these dialogues with sentences in Exercise 3.**

DIALOGUE 1:

A: _____

B: Do you think so? I'm not so sure. They still haven't found any proof that he was at the scene.

A: Yes, but who else could it be?

DIALOGUE 2:

A: I think you should stay and talk about it.

B: Well, _____ and I'm going.

A: Please don't!

DIALOGUE 3:

A: What do you think about the accused?

B: _____ .

A: But just because he hasn't broken the law before, it doesn't mean he isn't guilty.

DIALOGUE 4:

A: So how are you going to prove he was there?

B: _____

A: Well, if you have people who actually saw him, that would probably convince the jury.

STUDY SKILLS: summarising

1 Look back at the article on page 84. Answer these questions.

1 What is the main topic of the article?

_____

2 What is the information in the article based on?

_____

3 What are the main results reported?

_____

4 Which crimes are referred to?

_____

5 What is the overall message or conclusion of the article?

_____

2 Complete this summary of the article. See if you can use words from the article without looking at it again.

<u>Crime around the world</u>
Research shows that ¹_____ have
²_____ and more people than
³_____ can ⁴_____
around without ⁵_____ . For
example, ⁶_____ in the USA is at
one of its ⁷_____ ever but it has
risen a little in countries like ⁸_____
and ⁹_____ . Most countries say
there has been an ¹⁰_____ in the
number of ¹¹_____ of personal
theft. ¹²_____ has been
¹³_____ as one of the worst types
of ¹⁴_____ crime but it is lower
than in the ¹⁵_____ . This might be
because many ¹⁶_____ have better
¹⁷_____ . Car ¹⁸_____
is still worst in the ¹⁹_____ .

WRITING SKILLS: a narrative using cause and effect

3 Choose the correct linking words.

1 A burglar came into the offices last week. *Due to/ As a result*, we've installed new security devices.

2 He was behaving suspiciously *because/so* I stopped him and asked him what he was doing.

3 There was a terrorist alert. *Resulting/As a result* everyone was searched at the airport.

4 I was frightened at the stadium. *Due to/ Consequently*, I've never been back there.

5 I found blood on the stairs. *This caused/As a result* me to check upstairs in the bedroom.

6 There's a car crash in the centre of town. *The result/Because of this*, the road is closed.

7 *Because/Due to* the importance of the meeting between world leaders, we've increased the numbers of police around the building.

4 Look at these notes on causes and effects. Write full sentences with linkers.

1 too many people speeding ⟶ Government make new law (as a result…)

   As a result of too many people speeding, the
   Government have made a new law.

2 I'm ill ⟶ I'm off work today. (so…)

   _____

   _____

3 burglars stole jewels ⟶ police looking for green car (consequently…)

   _____

   _____

4 taxi crashed into bus ⟶ two people to be hurt (this caused…)

   _____

   _____

5 Poor sales of new product ⟶ high price (due to)

   _____

   _____

6 Very bad weather ⟶ trains cancelled (the result is…)

   _____

   _____

AUDIOSCRIPTS

CD 1

Lesson 1.2 Track 1.3

It obviously belongs to someone who walks into a room and likes everyone to know he's there. The way he uses the box tells me that he's quite sociable and outgoing. The signature looks fairly normal but the letters lean that way. If you combine that with the narrow gap between the words, then you have someone who is ambitious and self-confident. Finally, the way he finishes off the signature with the lines makes this person a real extrovert.

Lesson 1.3 Track 1.4

A: So I'd like to ask you a few questions about your TV habits. OK?

B: Sure.

A: First of all, what kind of TV programmes do you like?

B: Oh I don't watch that much. But I like the sport when it's on. Especially football.

A: Really? Who's your favourite player?

B: Ronaldhino.

A: Is he playing well at the moment?

B: Of course.

A: Are you a big fan?

B: Fairly.

A: What does he eat for breakfast?

B: I've no idea! I'm not that kind of fan. I just like watching him play.

A: Fine. How often do you go to the cinema?

B: Quite often.

A: Do you have any favourite actors or actresses?

B: Err. I like Johnny Depp movies. He's pretty cool. And I met him once! I went to the first night premiere of a film in London and he was there.

A: Interesting. Do you often go to see celebrities?

B: No, that was the only time. Oh actually I also went to meet Julia Roberts once…[fade]

Lesson 2.3 Track 1.9

Robert Byron was a British writer and he's famous because of his book, *The Road to Oxiana*. Many other travel writers have said it is the first example of great travel writing. Byron was born in 1905 and studied at Oxford. He also wrote about architecture but he is most famous for his travel writing. He published his first book, *First Russia, Then Tibet* in 1933. Then four years later, he wrote *The Road to Oxiana* about his ten-month journey to Afghanistan. The book won awards and people from all over the world have read it in different languages. After facing many dangers on his journeys, Byron died on a ship in the Second World War.

Lesson 2.4 Track 1.10

A: Have you thought any more about where to go on holiday?

B: Yes, I was reading about something called eco-tourism. I think we should do something like that. What do you think?

A: Well, I've read about that too, and there are arguments for and against.

B: What do you mean?

A: Well. On the one hand you fly to interesting places and help with projects, but on the other hand having lots of people travelling to parts of the world with ecological problems is probably causing more problems. Another disadvantage is that we don't have enough money to do that! It's quite expensive.

B: So, where should we go?

A: Well, I agree that it'd be a good idea to do something different rather than just sitting on a beach. How about going on an archaeological dig?

B: What's that exactly?

A: Well you travel to an ancient place and help dig for old buildings and objects. A friend of mine is working on one in the Sahara desert. I think we should join.

Lesson 3.1 Track 1.12

stressful

glamorous, challenging, flexible

exciting, rewarding

repetitive

Lesson 3.2 Track 1.13

Freida, Sandy

F: Hi Sandy.

S: Hi Frieda. Sorry I'm late. How long have you been waiting?

F: Not long. It's OK. I've been reading my book. It's about a detective. He's been chasing this bad guy for months. I've just got to the final chapter. Anyway, what've you been doing today?

S: I was with a friend. We've been studying for our exams. I still need to do much more!

F: What do you think you'll do after university?

S: I haven't spent any time on that yet. I just want to pass these exams first. What about you? How's the job?

F: Well, my company's been promising me a promotion for months but nothing's happened.

S: Well, you've been working there a long time. Maybe it's time to move on…

Lesson 3.4 Track 1.16

1 Q: What kind of person are you?

 A: I think I'm quite outgoing…

2 Q: What would you say is your biggest weakness?

 A: Probably, that I tend to take my work home, though some people call that a strength I suppose.

3 Q: What interests do you have outside work?

 A: I like cycling and visiting museums.

4 Q: If you were an animal what would it be?

 A: That's a difficult one... a leopard, perhaps.

5 Q: What do you think you can bring to this post?

A: Well, in my last job I learnt to use the latest technology.

6 Q: How much of a team player are you?

A: Well, I have plenty of experience of working with groups of people.

7 Q: How do you think your colleagues would describe you?

A: I think the people I work closely with would say I was supportive.

8 Q: Can you tell me about your qualifications?

A: Well, I have a degree in business studies and an MBA.

Lesson 4.2 Track 1.20

Teacher, Natalie

T: So, Natalie. You're a good language learner, so what techniques do you have for learning English? For example, when you meet a word for the first time what's the first thing you do?

N: I suppose if I know the meaning then I might say it a few times so I know how to say it properly.

T: Do you use a dictionary?

N: Sometimes. But I prefer to hear a word first if I can.

T: Great. And do you write it down or make a note of it?

N: Yes, I have a notebook that I keep all my new words in. After my English lesson I like to write up any words.

T: So what do you write?

N: I like to try and put it into my own language.

T: You mean translate it?

N: That's right.

T: And do you write a definition or anything like that?

N: Not usually, because my dictionary tells me that.

T: OK. Is there anything else you write down about the word?

N: One idea my friend told me was to write the new word in different ways. So if you learn a new word like manage, you also write words like manager or management.

T: Yes, that is a good idea. So how do you remember the words – because they might be in your notebook but can you use them?

N: Well, one technique I use is to write them on pieces of paper and test myself. That's a good way because I practise on the bus when I'm going to work…[fade]

Lesson 4.3 Track 1.22

A: If the Government doesn't spend more money on teaching languages then other languages might die out.

B: Yes, but if we teach school students these languages, there won't be time for important subjects like maths or science.

A: I agree that those subjects are also important, but in the future children will need to be bilingual in order to get a job. Besides, students at school won't just have to learn the language but could learn about cultures as well.

B: Yes that might help. But of course, if they want more language classes, it'll cost money.

A: That's ridiculous. It won't cost that much!

B: Besides if everyone speaks English, they don't need to learn any other languages.

Lesson 5.3 Track 1.26

Customer, Advertising agent

C: So what are you planning?

A: What we're planning is a new TV commercial that we'll show during sporting events like soccer matches. We'll also promote your company by sponsoring sport in schools.

C: That sounds great. So what will happen in the TV commercial?

A: Well, we'll try to get a famous soccer player to endorse the new brand of shoe. So we'll have camera shots of him playing and of course he'll wear the shoe which has your logo on the side.

C: Will we have some kind of catchy slogan?

A: Err maybe. Perhaps at the end of the advert the player will say something about the product which is easy to remember.

Lesson 5.4 Track 1.29

Chairman, Rose Joyce, Guest

One

C: Good morning everyone and thank you for coming. Our purpose today is to present plans for the new advertising campaign on the Internet. The presentation is divided into three parts. I'll begin with an overview of the target market and what kind of websites we are thinking of visiting. Then my colleague, Rose Joyce, will present some designs for banner ads and finally we'll take questions. If you have any questions during the talk, then feel free to ask… OK [fade]

Two

R: That brings us to the ads themselves. Please look at the screen. As you can see on this banner advertisement, we're keeping the company colour and the letters of the name are the same.

G: Excuse me, can I ask a question?

R: Sure, go ahead.

G: Why haven't you included the logo?

R: We feel that for this kind of advert the logo isn't necessary. Web users are more interested in images and photos – even moving things, and the logo just didn't fit in…[fade out]

Three

C: So that brings us to the end of the presentation. Are there any questions?

G: Yes, it's about your costs. They seem very high. I thought Internet advertising was supposed to be cheaper.

C: That's true in terms of production costs but you have to remember that there is much more time spent on finding suitable sites for the banner adverts. Also, market research is much more complex because you need to find out where different customers are going. On the other hand, this means that you can target your market more carefully.

G: But that still doesn't explain why…[fade out]

CD2

Lesson 6.1 Track 2.2

Bank manager, Customer

BM: So you intend to open your shop next month.

C: That's right.

BM: What kind of premises do you have?

C: Well, it's a small shop on the corner of a street. Towards the end of the high street near the bus station.

BM: I see. And what kind of funding do you have so far?

C: Well, my father has given me some and a couple of other family members. And I'll probably have to sell my house.

BM: And so how much do you want to borrow from the bank?

C: About fifty thousand.

BM: And when you forecast your profit and losses for the first year, how much of this do you think you can pay back per month?

C: About a thousand a month.

BM: But everyone knows that the first year is the hardest for attracting new customers. And your main competitors, the two big supermarkets outside the centre, also happen to be the market leaders. Don't you think they have all the customers already?

C: Ah yes, but I intend to begin by offering lots of discounts to get people to come to me. And besides, people like corner shops for things like milk and bread. It's a different type of market…[fade]

Lesson 6.3 Track 2.5

Gucci opened his first shop in Florence in 1920.

After a few years of working for himself, he had built a reputation for his leather craftsmanship and accessories.

Later, Guccio's four sons helped him run the firm.

In 1953 the first overseas shop opened in New York City.

In the same year Guccio died and he never saw the Gucci empire spread around the world.

His grandson, Maurizio (1949–1995) took over the business in the 1980s and enjoyed great success.

He became president of the company in 1989.

Following a series of legal and family problems, the company was sold off in 1993.

Lesson 6.4 Track 2.6

Italian salesman, American supplier

I: Hello, Prima Furnishings. Can I help you?

A: Hello, I'm calling from a company in the United States and we've been looking at your catalogue. We're thinking of placing a large order.

I: I see. Are you a supplier in the US?

A: Yes, we supply furniture stores. Especially slightly upmarket ones and we really like your range of lamps a great deal.

I: That's nice to hear. Were there any in particular?

A: We were thinking of ordering some of the Fatima lamps.

I: OK. So how many would you like to order?

A: Well, we think we'll need about three hundred.

I: Er… I'm afraid that would be a bit difficult. That's a large quantity. We wouldn't have that amount in stock.

A: I know, but the more we order the lower our shipping costs will be. What about if we paid earlier? So instead of payment on delivery we could pay – say 50 percent before. How do you feel about that?

I: Let me check if I understand you. You'd pay us half the amount before you receive them?

A: Yes, would you be able to do that?

I: That sounds fine. You know we could probably do something about the shipping costs as well…[fade]

Lesson 7.2 Track 2.9

A: The material for this must be very strong. We don't want it to break while people are carrying it around.

B: That's right. We shouldn't use metal because it's too heavy.

C: Yes I agree. If we use a strong plastic, we can make it in lots of different colours and it's also possible to make a rectangular shape.

A: Why rectangular? It doesn't have to look like all the competitors' designs, does it? I think we should try to come up with something new. We could make circular players for example.

B: True, but we mustn't produce something which people can't easily carry. The classic rectangular shape works because it's easy to put in your pocket.

C: Well, we can design a few versions and test them on consumers.

A: No, we can't because we don't have enough time before the launch next spring.

B: I know, but we shouldn't launch it until we're ready, otherwise it won't sell.

Lesson 9.1 Track 2.16

Student, Careers advisor

S: I'm thinking of going into engineering but I'm not sure if it's the right choice for me.

CA: Well, first of all, it's important to note that the term engineering can mean different things. For example, there's mechanical engineering which includes things like aerospace, the car industry or even building things for military use.

S: Well, really I'd like to do something that helps the environment.

CA: Well, there's environmental engineering. If you did that you'd be working in areas like finding ways to stop pollution from factories or how to clean up after an oil spill in the ocean. Do you like solving problems?

S: Yes, I suppose so.

CA: Well all engineers are problem-solvers. You'll also be really keen on building new things. I suppose you could say that environmental engineers spend a lot of time modifying mechanical inventions to make them environmentally friendly! [laughs].

Lesson 9.3 Track 2.17

The new tunnel will in fact be a set of three tubes, each of which will be 72 kilometres long in total. That's about one-and-a-half times longer than the Channel Tunnel between the United Kingdom and France. 52 kilometres of this will be under the sea, with the remaining 20 above ground and taking passengers to rail terminals at each end. The average depth of the undersea section will be 45 metres. We estimate that the average journey time through the tunnel by train will be about 25 minutes, travelling at around 160 kilometres per hour. The overall cost is currently thought to be in the region of 25 billion pounds.

Lesson 9.4 Track 2.19

A: What do you think about asking Malcolm Bernier who has just finished the Randalf Tower?

B: Great idea. Do you think he'd be free?

A: I don't know, but we can ask.

C: Sorry, but I don't think that's a good idea. His buildings are often criticised for being ugly.

A: Well, that's probably a good reason to invite him. The students will have lots of questions.

C: I don't know about that. And he isn't very good at talks. I saw him last month and he was very boring – and really unprepared.

B: What about inviting him and another designer so we can have some kind of debate?

A: That's a possible solution. What do you think about that?

C: Yes, let's do that. Much more interesting.

A: We all agree then. We'll do that.

B: Why don't we ask Lance Weiss? He was the one who built that famous bridge…

Lesson 10.2 Track 2.21

1

Those are new, aren't they? They're so cool. I love that new seventies retro look that everyone's wearing now. Do they fit you OK, they're not too tight?

2

Sorry, but I think I've lost it. It's got a black plastic strap and a white, metal face.

3

Audrey Hepburn looked great wearing them in all those old movies and now they've become such a beautiful, classic design. You can't walk anywhere in Italy without seeing someone in a cool, black pair whether the sun's shining or not.

4

It doesn't look like it'll be large enough for my photo. Also, I think a silver, metal one would look better than blue plastic. It wouldn't cost that much more.

5

We thought of getting plain, wooden ones but I think plastic are better for outside – when it rains or for bad weather. Anyway, they're very comfortable. I actually wanted green plastic ones but I could only get them in white.

Lesson 10.3 Track 2.22

Radio presenter, Doctor John Stivers

RP: Today I'm talking to Doctor John Stivers about living longer. Doctor Stivers, isn't it true that humans have always tried to live longer? So surely people talking about ways of living to a hundred is just a fashion.

DR JS: Yes, it's true that the human race has always tried to live longer – that's part of how humans have survived for so long. At a basic level we try to do this by avoiding danger but living longer also means we need to find a safe place to live. And of course plenty of food and a sense of belonging to a community – humans are very social, so being with others is part of survival and feeling healthy.

RP: So why are people living longer nowadays? Is it just because we have better cures for sickness?

DR JS: Well, that is the main reason. As humans we work towards medical advances and improving our houses and making life more comfortable – this all helps. And we seem to be successful. Figures show that the number of people who are living to a hundred is increasing every year. We estimate that there is currently one person in every 10,000 who is over one hundred.

RP: We often hear that women live longer than men. Is this still true?

DR JS: Yes, it's generally accepted, though medical science hasn't found real answers as to why. In fact, in recent years, the average lifespan for men has been catching up to that of women's.

RP: Really? That is interesting. So, what advice would you have for anyone wishing to live longer?

DR JS: Well, I'm sure anyone listening will have heard most of them before. Eat well, so… lots of fruit and vegetables. Few overweight people live to be a hundred and obviously smokers tend to die before a hundred. Then there are other factors. People who are a hundred are good at dealing with stress and optimistic, and also tend not to be poor. I don't mean they have to be rich but they have some money and financial security.

RP: So you're saying we can control whether we live longer or not.

DR JS: Not entirely. Everyday there is new research into the genes in our bodies and scientists have found that some of us are programmed from birth to live longer.

RP: And finally, are there any problems with living longer? Perhaps not everyone wants to live to a hundred

DR JS: That's the question more and more people – and governments – are asking. I think people who worry about living longer are in danger of not enjoying the present. And just because you live to 101, it doesn't mean that you will also be healthy.

Lesson 10.4 Track 2.24

A: Good morning everyone. We're here to discuss the facilities for older people at the beach. Who would like to begin?

B: I would. I'm very unhappy that we have to pay to get to the beach. It doesn't help that the car park is a fifteen-minute walk from the beach…

A: Please make your point.

B: Well, it isn't acceptable that we should pay. It should be free for pensioners to get on to the beach.

A: I see how you feel. Thank you for your comment. I'll look into the matter.

C: Sorry, can I just say something please?

A: Sure. Go ahead…[fade]

Lesson 11.3 Track 2.26

Interviewer, Marlene

I: Hello, Marlene. You've just finished your first TV show. Do you think you'll do another?

M: I'll take some time off first.

I: Why's that? Didn't you enjoy it?

M: No. I loved doing the show but I need a break.

I: Does that mean you are having a break from fashion modelling as well?

M: No. In fact I'm going to Milan for a clothes photo shoot next week.

I: I see. So has the TV show changed your life?

M: No, it hasn't, though more people recognise me in the street and try to say hello and touch me.

I: Does that bother you?

M: Yes, it does, a bit. I used to be able to go to the supermarket but last week I'd just paid for my shopping when a newspaper photographer took my picture.

I: Do you get tired of the cameras?

M: No, never. I've been doing this kind of thing for five years. If I don't like it, I'll have to become a recluse I suppose.

Lesson 11.4 Track 2.27

M: So what do you fancy this evening?

W: Nothing violent. I don't want you to get any more of those films with endless fight scenes and awful acting.

M: How about this one?

W: But that's by the same director.

M: Yes, but it's very different from his others.

W: Well, the front looks very similar with all those people fighting. How about a nice romantic comedy? I haven't seen this one before.

M: We must be able to find something much better than that. It'll just be lots of kissing in fields. What's this?

W: It's that TV series about global warming. It's beautifully filmed but I'd rather watch something less serious this evening.

M: This looks good. It's set on a spaceship and slowly everyone disappears.

W: I suppose we could do a lot worse than that. I do like the actress in it.

Lesson 11.5 Track 2.28

Good morning Ladies and Gentlemen and thank you for coming. The purpose of today's meeting is to update you on the university's open day. I've divided the meeting into two parts. Firstly, I'll tell you about the plans and then, we'll discuss who is in charge of what. Feel free to ask any questions at any stage…[fade]

Lesson 12.3 Track 2.31

Newsreader: And now local news. Members of a bank were held hostage for over three hours this morning as police tried to convince the robber to give himself up. Nigel Low, aged 29, pointed a gun at staff and told them to give him the money behind the desks. A member of staff managed to press the emergency button and police arrived in minutes. Low eventually gave himself up and no-one was hurt. The gun turned out to be a toy. Meanwhile, in the case of the Dublin boy who hacked into computers, it was the turn of the prosecutor today to talk to witnesses about the character of the boy. One witness described him as 'a nice boy who would never hurt anyone.' The case continues.

Lesson 12.4 Track 2.32

Members of the jury, the facts of this case are simple but let me summarise the main facts for you one more time so there is no doubt in your minds. At 9 p.m. on a Sunday evening, Kerry Kane entered the garage and pulled out a gun. He told the cashier to give him the money. Half an hour later he was caught by the police with £2010. There should be no doubts in your minds that this man is guilty. However, you have to decide the punishment to fit this crime. You can look at it in two ways. You can see Mr Kane as a dangerous criminal who should have been taken off our streets months ago. Or you can see Mr Kane as a victim of his childhood. A man with no close relationships and repeated bad behaviour at school.

Lesson 2.2 Ex 3

Quiz answers:

1 B

2 A

3 C

4 A

5 C

Lesson 9.3 Exercise 2

1 a

2 a

3 c

4 b

5 b

6 b

7 a

8 c

9 a

10 b

Unit 1 Lesson 1

1

1 sensible
2 ambitious
3 cautious
4 assertive
5 talkative
6 bossy
7 creative
8 organised

2a

1 ad<u>ven</u>turous
2 easy-<u>go</u>ing
3 am<u>bit</u>ious
4 even-<u>tem</u>pered
5 <u>cau</u>tious
6 open-<u>min</u>ded
7 ener<u>get</u>ic
8 <u>or</u>ganised
9 re<u>li</u>able
10 self-<u>con</u>fident
11 <u>gen</u>erous
12 cre<u>at</u>ive

3

1 insensitive
2 unambitious
3 impatient
4 unsociable
5 unreliable

Unit 1 Lesson 2

4

Signature 1: Mostly b)
Signature 2: Mostly a)
Signature 3: Mostly c)

5

Signature 1: an A person

7

1 How
2 What
3 Have
4 Do
5 Where
6 Why
7 Are
8 Does
9 What
10 How
11 When
12 Is

8

1 Who was Carl Jung?
2 Where did he study medicine?
3 What did he specialise in?
4 What did he develop?
5 How many personality types did he identify?
6 Who don't (doesn't) like crowds?
7 What do extroverts do/form?
8 How influential was Jung?
9 Which (personality) tests are based on his theory?
10 Which filmmaker read his work?
11 What did he interpret?
12 Which book did he write in 1957?

Unit 1 Lesson 3

1

1 anti
2 under
3 ex
4 dis
5 mis
6 mono
7 over
8 semi
9 dis
10 re
11 out
12 under
13 in
14 bi

2

1 do you do
2 start
3 makes
4 compares
5 is probably giving
6 are reading
7 's also trying
8 runs

3

I'm working in the office at the moment but my boss always has lunch at 12 so I'm writing to you while he's out. Are you having a good time in Barcelona at the moment? What do you think of your course? How's the weather? It's raining here!

4

1 has
2 believe
3 is going up
4 are becoming
5 take
6 shows
7 has (have)
8 think
9 are beginning
10 replace

5

1 c
2 e
3 a
4 b
5 d

6

1 What kind of TV programmes do you like?
2 Who's your favourite player?
3 Is he playing well at the moment?
4 Are you a big fan?
5 What does he eat for breakfast?
6 How often do you go to the cinema?
7 Do you have any favourite actors or actresses?
8 Do you often go to see celebrities?

Unit 1 Lesson 4

1

1 g
2 h
3 b
4 a
5 f
6 d
7 e
8 c

2

1 Why don't we employ Magda?
2 I suggest we call him and see if he wants the job.
3 How about giving them all a team task?
4 What about checking their references before we decide?
5 What do you think about Petra?
6 I agree with Michael.

3a

1 c
2 b
3 b
4 c
5 c
6 a
7 a

Unit 1 Lesson 5

1

1 $200,000
2 speeches
3 between 9 and 10 million dollars
4 350 talks
5 combat HIV/Aids.

2

1 However
2 Although
3 example
4 Despite
5 because
6 contrast
7 sum
8 balance

3

1 d
2 b

3 f
4 a
5 g
6 c
7 e

Unit 2 Lesson 1

1

2

1 broaden
2 explore
3 find
4 get
5 become
6 see
7 respect
8 find out

3

1 insurance policy
2 travel agent
3 holiday resort
4 Dress codes
5 package tour

Unit 2 Lesson 2

1

4 5 1   7   3 9 6   8   2

1940   1964   1972 1977   1989

2

1 set out
2 stop off
3 get to
4 get back
5 look around
6 carry on

3

1 check in
2 check out
3 get in
4 take off
5 stop over
6 pull over

4

1 started
2 left
3 followed
4 walked
5 found
6 was
7 photographed
8 went
9 continued
10 became

5

1 reached (B)
2 led (A)
3 became (C)
4 sailed (A)
5 made (C)

6a

1 in-vent-ed 3
2 danced 1
3 dis-cussed 2
4 dec-id-ed 3
5 trav-elled 2
6 a-rrived 2
7 in-trod-uced 3
8 land-ed 2
9 worked 1
10 lift-ed 2

7

We travelled across the desert for another week and then began to climb mountains. During this time, one of our team began to feel sick. We carried him but the journey was slow. Then, two days later, some people found us and took us to their tents. They lived in the desert. Their leader was an old man and he brought medicine to us. We didn't know what the medicine was but after a week our friend was better. The people in the desert gave us more food and water and we set out once again into the heat and the sun.

Unit 2 Lesson 3

1

1 d
2 f
3 a
4 c
5 g
6 b
7 e

3

1 have you been
2 spoke
3 've just returned
4 flew
5 walked
6 've never done
7 took

8 invited
9 spent
10 didn't spend
11 bought
12 've already booked

4

1 I travelled all night.
2 He climbed this mountain.
3 They've worked here for years.
4 She's told him the news
5 We talked to them.
6 It hit the building.

5

1 was
2 told
3 took
4 began
5 filmed
6 stopped
7 survived
8 swum
9 has also swum
10 was
11 packed
12 took

6

1 did explorers tell us about their adventures
2 did Martin Strel take with him
3 did the camera men film
4 did these sections of river stop in the past
5 did his back-up team pack animal food

7

1 F   2 F   3 T   4 F   5 T
6 T   7 F

8

1 Many other travel writers.
2 In 1905.
3 In 1933.
4 Four years later.
5 The road to Oxiana.

Unit 2 Lesson 4

1

1 b
2 b
3 a
4 c
5 a

2

1 b
2 f
3 e
4 d
5 c
6 a
7 g

3

1 we should
2 arguments for and against
3 one hand
4 other hand
5 disadvantage
6 a good idea to
7 How
8 think

Unit 2 Lesson 5

1

1 Amelia Earhart was born in Kansas.
2 She attended Columbia University in nineteen nineteen.
3 She went to her first air show in nineteen twenty.
4 Her first record was to fly at fourteen thousand feet.
5 Most people remember her as the first woman to fly solo non-stop across the Atlantic.
6 She took off from New Brunswick.
7 She published two books about her experiences.

2

1 writer
2 1905
3 Studied
4 architecture
5 travel
6 Died / a ship
7 Russia
8 Tibet
9 Road

3

1 After
2 Before
3 During
4 when
5 after
6 while
7 when
8 while
9 before
10 during

4

3 But before I had finished my first year, I decided to leave and travel.
2 While we were living there, I started a degree in business at the university.
4 In 2003, during a trek in the Himalayas, I met my wife, Angela.
5 After we had finished our journey round the world together, we started an online tourist business, specialising in tourism to exotic places.
1 In 1995 my family moved to Brussels when my father took a job there.

Unit 3 Lesson 1

1

1 rewarding
2 challenging
3 glamorous
4 stressful
5 repetitive
6 flexible

exciting is the extra word

2

Oo   stressful
Ooo   glamorous, challenging, flexible
oOo   rewarding, exciting
oOoo   repetitive

4

1 for
2 for
3 to
4 in
5 of
6 on
7 for
8 in

Unit 3 Lesson 2

1

1 a
2 c
3 a
4 b
5 c
6 a
7 b
8 a
9 c
10 b

2

1 b
2 b
3 c
4 a

4

1 b   2 c   3 c   4 c   5 a

5a

1 have I been waiting
2 've been reading
3 has been chasing
4 have I been doing
5 have been studying
6 has been promising
7 have been working

6

1 since
2 since
3 for
4 since
5 for
6 since
7 since
8 for

7

Interviewer, Candidate

I: So in your current job I see that you've mainly been working from home. How long have you been doing that?
C: Well, I've been working for my employer for about three and a half years but after a couple of years I was able to begin doing some of my work at home.
I: So, how's it been going? I mean, have you been enjoying it?
C: Actually, it's one of the reasons I'd like to change jobs. I love my work but I miss working in a team. That's one of the things which has attracted me to this post.
I: So if we offered you the chance to work from home, you wouldn't take it?
C: Well, obviously if the job required it, then that would be fine. But I'd really prefer to work alongside people. I think that's one of my strengths – my ability to communicate.

Unit 3 Lesson 3

1

1 d
2 f
3 b
4 e
5 a
6 c

2

1 F
2 T
3 F
4 F
5 F
6 T

3

shock tactics
contact details
survey results
past experince
killer question
customer services
recruitment agency
smart appearance

4

1 contact details
2 survey results
3 killer question
4 shock tactics
5 past experience
6 customer services

7 recruitment agency
8 smart appearance

5

1 've done
2 've been doing
3 've replied
4 's been talking
5 have you spent
6 have you been waiting
7 used
8 complained
9 's broken
10 have applied

6

1 all day
2 in the last three weeks
3 in the last hour
4 for days
5 at the interview
6 years
7 in three hours
8 8 o'clock this morning

7a

1 We've been here for hours. (6)
2 I've interviewed three people. (5)
3 She's been interviewing all week. (6)
4 They've had their interview. (5)
5 He's been employed as a manager. (7)
6 You've always worked as a teacher. (7)
7 It's been going wrong for days. (7)

8

1 How long have you been writing that report?
2 How many reports have you written?
3 Have you been waiting a long time?
4 Where has he lived?
5 Where have they been living?
6 Who has she been interviewing all morning?
7 How many have they interviewed this morning?

Unit 3 Lesson 4

1

recruit more staff
deal with complaints (customers)
research new markets
set objectives
serve customers
put together a plan
reduce costs
lead a team

2

1 b
2 g
3 f
4 a
5 d

6 e
7 c

3

1 glad
2 question
3 detail
4 moment
5 ask
6 expert
7 honest

4

1 person
2 weakness
3 interests
4 animal
5 bring
6 team
7 colleagues
8 qualifications

5

f 1
a 2
g 3
c 4
b 5
h 6
e 7
d 8

Unit 3 Lesson 5

1

Paragraph 1: 1 e 2 g 3 h 4 b
Paragraph 2: 5 f 6 a 7 c 8 d

2

1 I *'m* writing to apply for the post of trainee journalist,
2 *which* you advertised in this morning's newspaper.
3 I have always been interested *in* current affairs and
4 local politics and I *would* like the opportunity to report on them.
5 I am *an* outgoing, confident person with good
6 communication skills. In *my* spare time I have also run
7 the student newsletter *at* my university.
8 I am available at *a (any)* time convenient to you for an
9 interview, where I look forward *to* discussing my application.

3

Dear Sir/Madam

I am writing to apply for the post of summer school activities leader as advertised in the student magazine.

I have been interested in outdoor activities for many years and in my

spare time I like rock-climbing and team sports.

I am an outgoing person with good leadership skills and am good with teenagers.

I am available any time for an interview. I look forward to meeting you to discuss my application.

Yours faithfully,

Unit 4 Lesson 1

1

1 slang
2 accent
3 native speakers
4 grammar
5 foreign languages
6 bilingual
7 dialect

2

1 lets
2 catch
3 falling
4 picks
5 get
6 take
7 keep

3b

1 I can't keep‿up with the class.
2 Take‿up‿a hobby.
3 He catches‿on well.
4 She has‿a foreign‿accent.
5 I'm learning to drive‿a car.
6 Can‿I learn‿it‿easily?

Unit 4 Lesson 2

1

1 They're going to do
2 I'll call you.
3 People won't stop
4 I'll probably see you
5 We're meeting at three
6 She's going to join us
7 When are you returning from Beijing?/ When will you be returning from Beijing?
8 Sorry, I'm not going to work here

2

1 a prediction about the future: 3
2 a decision made at the time of speaking: 2
3 an intention for the future: 1 (6, 8)
4 a fixed arrangement, plan or programme: 5

3

1 'm going to apply
2 'll probably leave
3 're meeting

4 'll ask
5 'm going
6 'll do
7 will use
8 's picking
9 are going to sell
10 'll see

4a

1 She's going to leave at five. (6)
2 I'll go now if that's OK. (6)
3 I am going after lunch. (5)
4 We're meeting in a minute. (5)
5 They'll call you back at eight. (6)
6 He's catching the train tonight. (5)
7 It will work if we make it work. (8)
8 You're going to do it, aren't you? (7)

5

1 let
2 permit
3 allow
4 allow
5 permitted
6 Let

6

1 look it up
2 write them up (note them down)
3 write them out (write them up)
4 read them out
5 read up on it
6 note them down

7

1 c
2 b
3 a
4 c
5 a

9

New research figures show that we sent just over 3 billion text messages last month. This figure was up by twenty-five percent on May and beat the previous monthly record of two point five billion texts sent in March. One representative for the research company said that texting is going to become the normal form of communication for all mobile phone users. She also predicted that we will send almost 40 billion texts this year. That will mean figures are up by nearly a third on last year.

Unit 4 Lesson 3

1

1 spends
2 won't be
3 work
4 'll pass
5 get
6 'll arrive

7 won't cost
8 study

2

1 'll see
2 arrive
3 don't use
4 will start
5 don't ask
6 won't come
7 see
8 will you study

3a

1 The Government.
2 Bilingual
3 Culture
4 Language classes

3b

1 might die out
2 get a job
3 other cultures
4 maths and science
5 costs extra money
6 everyone speaks English

4a

1 If we spend any more money, we won't have any left.

2 If we teach languages, they'll become bilingual.

3 Students won't have time for maths, if we teach English.

4 We don't need to learn a language, if everyone else speaks English.

5

1 F
2 T
3 F
4 T
5 T
6 F
7 F

6

There are five sentences in the first conditional:

'If more money and resources aren't given to traditional foreign language classrooms in the USA, some people believe languages such as French or German might die out.'

'If we offer an American Sign Language (ASL), we'll have enough students for three courses.'

'Unless colleges offer these kinds of courses, deaf people will never really be part of society.'

'If ASL is equal to traditional languages, it will have the same number of words and emotional range.'

'If you understand and use sign language, you'll understand the world the same as in any other language.'

Unit 4 Lesson 4

1

1 I don't know about that.
2 If we do that, it will cause some problems.
3 I think you're right.
4 I think that would work.
5 I'm afraid I don't like that idea.
6 It's definitely worth considering.
7 I'm not sure about that.
8 What will happen if we do that?

3

1 will happen if we do that
2 I don't like that idea
3 think you're right
4 know about that
5 if we do that
6 that would work

4a

A: I read a report that says if children learn a language from the age of four, it improves their intelligence. Do you think we should introduce Spanish classes for the younger pupils?
B: It's definitely worth considering. If we have lessons, it will make them bilingual more quickly.
A: Yes, I think you're right. Let's do that. And we could also buy some computer programs for them to use during the lessons.
B: I don't know about that. These computer programs can be a lot of money.
A: Well, I agree that it will be expensive initially, but once we've bought the software we can use it with the children year after year. And they like using the computers. I also thought we could start an after-school Spanish club. We'd have games and songs in Spanish for anyone interested. What do you think?
B: Yes, I think that would work. A lot of
· kids would really enjoy it.
A: I'm glad you like the idea.

Unit 4 Lesson 5

1

1 over
2 under

3 fifth
4 half
5 exactly
6 approximately
7 more
8 fifths
9 almost
10 well

2

1 a half of
2 a third
3 a third
4 a quarter
5 a fifth
6 a third/third
7 a quarter

3

The two charts show the percentages of students learning foreign languages in school five years ago and last year. The language with the biggest increase of 20 percent has been Spanish. In addition, Chinese has also increased by 9 percent. However, the number of students learning French and German have decreased by 20 percent and 9 percent.

Unit 5 Lesson 1

1

1 grabbing
2 catching
3 catchy
4 strong
5 attention
6 desire
7 action
8 persuasive
9 original
10 exotic

3a

pers<u>ua</u>sive
a<u>tt</u>ention
pro<u>mote</u>
s<u>pon</u>sorship
co<u>mm</u>ercial
ex<u>o</u>tic
en<u>dorse</u>
s<u>lo</u>gan
e<u>ff</u>ective
<u>lo</u>go
de<u>sire</u>
mis<u>lea</u>ding

Unit 5 Lesson 2

1

1 word-of-mouth
2 poster
3 TV commercials
4 leaflet

5 radio spot
6 endorsement
7 side of bus

2

1 b
2 c
3 a
4 b
5 b
6 a
7 c

3

1 cachet
2 privilege
3 subtle
4 a downturn
5 scene
6 blurred
7 sacrificed
8 global appeal

4

1 would ('d) choose
2 had
3 gave
4 were (was)
5 would ('d) happen
6 had
7 wouldn't receive
8 wouldn't buy

5

1 will know
2 knew
3 'll get
4 would give
5 'll pay
6 would happen
7 will be
8 will do

Unit 5 Lesson 3

1

1 Advertising managers
2 interactive website
3 persuasive message
4 attractive target
5 Media analysis
6 junk food
7 fast food
8 vast sums

2

1 better
2 most worrying
3 fatter
4 shorter
5 later
6 most effective
7 worse
8 wider
9 more persuasive
10 more aware

3

1 a funny as
  b funnier than
2 a strictest
  b as strict as
3 a the tastiest
  b as tasty as

4

1 TV commercial
2 sporting events
3 soccer matches
4 sponsoring sport in schools
5 endorse the new brand
6 logo on the side.
7 is easy to remember.

5a

1 Mark's as tall as Michael. /ə/ /ə/ /ə/
2 Coffee tastes better than tea. /ə/ /ə/ /ə/
3 It's a lot faster. /ə/ /ə/
4 We're sellers of soft drinks. /ə/ /ə/
5 Is it as expensive? /ə/

6

Philips Electronics: Let's make things better.

Duracell: No battery is stronger longer.

Apple Computers: Everything is easier on a Mac.

Pfizer pharmaceuticals: Working for a healthier world.

Country Life butter: You'll never put a better bit of butter on your knife.

Nescafe: Coffee at its best.

Maltesers (chocolates): The lighter way to enjoy chocolate.

Disneyland: The happiest place on Earth

Dodge Trucks: Bigger in Texas, Better in a Dodge

Unit 5 Lesson 4

1

1 c
2 e
3 g
4 a
5 f
6 j
7 i
8 d
9 h
10 b

2

Good morning everyone and thank you for coming.

ANSWER KEY

Our purpose today is to

The presentation is divided into three parts.

If you have any questions

Please look at the screen.

So that brings us to the end of the presentation.

Are there any questions?

3

> *Purpose of presentation*
>
> To present plans for the new advertising campaign on THE INTERNET
>
> THREE parts to presentation:
> — Overview of the target market and websites
> — DESIGNS FOR BANNER ADS
> — Questions
>
> *Design of banner ads:*
> — the company colour WON'T change
> — the letters of the name won't change
> — the logo WON'T appear on ANY adverts
>
> *Costs*
> — Internet advertising is LESS expensive than TV in terms of production costs
> — You need more time to find good sites for the adverts.
> — Internet advertising allows you to sell to customers more carefully.

Unit 5 Lesson 5

1
1 a
2 b
3 a
4 c
5 a
6 b
7 b
8 b

2
verb + preposition:
enquire about
succeed in
complain about
show on
apologise for
look forward to
adjective + preposition:
horrified by
interested in
noun + preposition:
problem with
information about
law against
complaint about

3
1 enquire about
2 information about
3 horrified by
4 show/on
5 complain about
6 problem with
7 apologise for
8 look forward to

Unit 6 Lesson 1

1
charge high prices
make a profit
make a loss
pay low wages
break the law
avoid paying
invest in the local community
value your staff

2
1 charge high prices
2 make a loss
3 avoid paying
4 value your staff
5 invest in the local community
6 break the law
7 pay low wages
8 make a profit

3
1 customer
2 entrepreneur
3 partner
4 retailers
5 wholesaler
6 manufacturer

4
1 small shop
2 money/funding
3 his house
4 fifty thousand
5 forecast
6 thousand
7 market leaders
8 discounts
9 get people to come to him

Unit 6 Lesson 2

1
1 c
2 d
3 f
4 b
5 g
6 a
7 e

2
1 was working
2 noticed
3 was becoming

4 switched
5 was eating
6 began
7 was just wondering
8 threw
9 was trying
10 saw
11 was asking
12 were

3
1 saw
2 was/were offering
3 went
4 were also buying
5 bought
6 was still waiting
7 heard
8 were also waiting
9 took
10 got

4a
1 We were busy when it rang.
2 I was in another part of the building.
3 Was he with you?
4 He said they were.
5 Were they waiting for us?
6 She was late as usual.
7 Nina was talking to someone.
8 Yes, it was.

5
Here is the news. Today shops and supermarkets were sending jars of peanut butter back after the U.S. food safety authority said that customers had become ill while they were eating the product. At first the authority was only asking for jars of peanut butter bought since May 2006. However, by last night they were saying that all jars from October 2004 with the product code 2111 were dangerous. Public relations representatives from the food company were desperately trying to stop an even bigger PR disaster this morning. One manager said that no other food products were affected and customers should not be worried.

Unit 6 Lesson 3

1
1 run
2 profit/make
3 launch
4 found
5 bankrupt
6 negotiate
7 product

3
Gucci opened his first shop in Florence in 1920.

After a few years of working for himself, he had built a reputation for his leather craftsmanship and accessories.

Later, Guccio's four sons helped him run the firm.

In 1953 the first overseas shop opened in New York City.

In the same year Guccio died and he never saw the Gucci empire spread around the world.

His grandson, Maurizio (1949–1995), took over the business in the 1980s and enjoyed great success.

He became president of the company in 1989.

Following a series of legal and family problems, the company was sold off in 1993.

5

1 manage
2 manager
3 manufacture
4 manufacturer
5 competition
6 competitor
7 employ
8 employment
9 advertise
10 advertising/advertisement/advert
11 supply
12 supplier

6

1 manager
2 manufacturing
3 management
4 advertisement
5 employ
6 competitors
7 supplier('s)
8 manufacture
9 employment
10 advertise
11 supply
12 manufacturer/s

7

1 was born
2 had been
3 had left
4 started
5 founded
6 was launching
7 were selling
8 launched
9 moved

8

1 had been
2 started
3 closed
4 had planned
5 'd made /went

Unit 6 Lesson 4

1

1 The United States.
2 From their catalogue.
3 A supplier of furniture stores.
4 Their Fatima lamps.
5 Three hundred.
6 They don't have that amount in stock.
7 It reduces shipping costs.
8 50% of the payment before delivery.

2a

1 How many would you like to order?
2 We are thinking of placing a large order.
3 I'm afraid that would be a bit difficult.
4 What about if we paid earlier?
5 How do you feel about that?
6 Let me check if I understand you.
7 Would you be able to do that?
8 That sounds fine.

3a

1 I'm afraid he's out.
2 That will be really difficult for us.
3 We're thinking of placing a large order.
4 That sounds great!
5 I'm so sorry but I can't.
6 How many would you like?
7 Did you say a hundred?
8 Can you deliver by tomorrow?

4

	1	Q	U	A	N	T	I	T	Y	
2	P	A	Y	M	E	N	T			
	3	B	A	R	G	A	I	N		
4	D	I	S	C	O	U	N	T		
5	P	R	O	F	I	T				
	6	D	E	L	I	V	E	R	Y	
		7	R	A	N	G	E			
	8	R	E	T	A	I	L	E	R	
9	O	R	D	E	R					

Unit 6 Lesson 5

1

1 c
2 f
3 d
4 a
5 b
6 e
7 h
8 g

2

1 Dear Mr Smith
2 With reference to your previous email…
3 I would be delighted to meet you next week.

4 If you wish, I would also be happy to give you a tour of the factory.
5 I look forward to seeing you.
6 Yours sincerely

a Hi Jake
b Good to hear from you.
c The party sounds great – I'd love to come.
d Shall I bring anything?
e See you there.
f All the best

3 (Suggested answers)

1 Dear customer
2 I am writing to inform you about a change on our website
3 I am delighted to tell you that you can now order online.
4 We would be grateful if you could register within the next two weeks.
5 Do not hesitate to email me if you need any assistance with this.
6 I look forward to speaking to you soon.
7 Yours sincerely.

Unit 7 Lesson 1

1

1 designer
2 scientific
3 manufacturer/s
4 productive
5 user
6 development
7 innovative
8 invention
9 artist
10 engineer

2

1 traditional
2 futuristic
3 mass-produced
4 elegant
5 streamlined
6 hand-made
7 innovative
8 retro

Unit 7 Lesson 2

1

1 Streamlining
2 optimism
3 modernity
4 consumerism
5 industrialisation
6 efficiency
7 Ergonomics
8 Recycling
9 innovation

2a

1 O o o

ANSWER KEY

2 O o o o
3 o O o o
4 o O o o o
5 o O o o o o O o
6 o O o o

3a

1 Personal music player; MP3 player.
2 Metal, strong plastic.
3 Rectangular, circular.
4 To test on consumers.
5 Next spring.

3b

1 strong
2 metal
3 a strong plastic
4 shape
5 designs
6 pocket/s
7 versions
8 launch

4

1 's possibly
2 aren't able
3 's advisable
4 's important/'s essential
5 's important/'s essential
6 's not advisable
7 isn't possible
8 's advisable
9 aren't able
10 's possible

5a

1 a
2 b
3 a
4 a
5 a
6 c
7 b
8 a
9 c
10 b

Unit 7 Lesson 3

1

1 e
2 b
3 f
4 a
5 d
6 c

2

1 must
2 not possible
3 can't
4 might
5 can't
6 must
7 Perhaps
8 certain

3

Streamlining in design began in the nineteen thirties. Designers increased the efficiency of transport and this influenced the design of other products. Consumers wanted designs which suggested modernity. Later in the sixties, design reflected the new optimism of the period and the rise of the throwaway society. The period saw new materials and new shapes and colours and design. Later in the century, there was a reaction against the throwaway culture and the damage caused by industrialisation. Designers knew they must use energy-saving materials and products with a focus on durability.

4

1 A
2 C
3 B
4 A
5 C
6 A
7 B
8 C
9 A
10 B

Unit 7 Lesson 4

1a

_2_ Today I'd like to present this new design.
_4_ However, the elegant handle is made completely of metal.
_1_ Good morning everyone and thanks for coming.
_5_ Because of this, one of the best points is that it's unlikely to break when you use it.
_7_ I'd expect that it would appeal to anyone who enjoys a glass of wine with their dinner.
_6_ At £5.50 it's excellent value for money and…
_3_ As you can see it looks very similar to the old wooden design.

a corkscrew

2a

1 It looks very stylish.
2 It has several qualities.
3 That's a special feature.
4 It has a metallic base.
5 It's excellent value for money.
6 It's made of a strong plastic.

3

 triangle   circle
square rectangle
 cube sphere

4

1 triangular
2 circular
3 square
4 rectangular
5 cubic
6 spherical

5

1 triangular
2 square
3 circular
4 rectangular
5 cubic
6 spherical

Unit 7 Lesson 5

1

1 Dear Ray
2 I'm writing about the attachment you sent with
3 the two designs. I really like the first one
4 which is made of wood. It looks very
5 stylish but not very functional. The second
6 might be better because it's easy to use but
7 it isn't very innovative. How about combining
8 the appearance of the first and the practicality of
9 the second? Please send me your new
10 design by Thursday.

3

1 Also
2 Consequently
3 On the other hand
4 As a result
5 Moreover
6 Although

4

1 Although
2 Moreover
3 consequently
4 On the other hand
5 also
6 However

Unit 8 Lesson 1

1

1 Compulsory
2 private
3 Higher
4 primary

5 Continuous
6 secondary
7 Nursery

3
1 c
2 f
3 b
4 e
5 a
6 d

4
1 a
2 c
3 a
4 b
5 c
6 c
7 b

Unit 8 Lesson 2

1
1 friendly
2 easy-going
3 strict
4 punctual
5 well-prepared
6 pace
7 unique
8 criticised

2
1 Elementary education
2 higher education
3 continuous assessment
4 compulsory education
5 graduates
6 failed

3
1 pupil
2 raincoat
3 lessons
4 teachers
5 concentrate
6 fresh air
7 staff
8 parents
9 happier
10 enthusiastic

4
1 who
2 which
3 whose
4 where
5 when

5
1 He's a professor who works at a
   university in London.
2 Exams are a requirement which take
   place every summer.

3 A teacher is a person whose job is to
   show students how to learn, as well
   as what to learn.
4 The mid-morning break is a period in
   the school day when pupils relax and
   change classrooms.
5 Grades are marks that are often given
   for homework.
6 Nursery is a place where children
   aged 1–5 go.

6
1 Students who miss school sometimes
   fail their exams.
2 The school (where) I study at is a
   mixed-sex school.
3 Speak to the teacher who is in charge
   of sports.
4 Children who read with their parents
   for 30 minutes a day at home do very
   well at school.
5 This isn't the homework (which/that) I
   did.
6 The bag (which/that) I left in the
   classroom is brown.

7a
1 go
2 real
3 fact
4 paid
5 life
6 retake
7 university
8 when

Unit 8 Lesson 3

1
1 c
2 f
3 a
4 e
5 b

2
1 myth
2 fake
3 accredited
4 accelerated
5 flexibility
6 interact

3
1 T
2 F
3 F
4 F
5 T

4
1 d
2 f
3 a
4 c
5 b

6 e
7 g

6
1 My school, which won an award last
   year, is a secondary school.
2 Mr Sanders, who runs the maths
   department, is my favourite teacher.
3 The library, which was built in 1808,
   has over fifty thousand books.
4 My university, which is one of the
   most modern in the country, is
   famous for science and research.
5 The students, who were
   demonstrating against the
   government cuts in education,
   walked peacefully through the city
   centre.

Unit 8 Lesson 4

1
1 outstanding
2 well-stocked
3 spacious
4 break down
5 state-of-the-art
6 well run
7 standard

2

Where are you thinking of studying
this year? Come to Riverside College
where our outstanding teaching staff are
waiting to help you. Our ninety-nine
per cent pass rate, which is based on
results from the last five years, makes us
one of the top colleges in the country.
You'll be amazed at the progress you
make in such a short time. You'll enjoy
doing research in the well-run library
and using the state-of-the-art media
facilities. And when you want to relax
there's our spacious campus with
beautiful views and walks. Call us now
on 08003445295 for a free brochure or
visit us on www.riversidecollege.com

3
1 ways
2 options
3 advantage
4 things
5 way
6 what
7 thing
8 now

4
1 sentence 8
2 sentence 1
3 sentence 3
4 sentence 7
5 sentence 5

Unit 8 Lesson 5

1

a Scanning
b Skimming

2

1 Five.
2 Face-to-face and online learning.
3 For.
4 That employers won't accept degrees from these schools.
5 Flexibility.
6 Your country's educational bodies.

3

1 asking
2 full
3 wait
4 sign up
5 Best wishes
6 more
7 happy
8 Hi
9 thank you
10 pick
11 put inside
12 good

4

1 Dear
2 grateful for
3 comprehensive
4 As you will
5 enclosed
6 fee
7 Please
8 suitable
9 Should you
10 hesitate
11 I look forward to hearing
12 Best

Unit 9 Lesson 1

1

1 civil
2 aerospace
3 biomedical
4 mechanical
5 computer

3

1 engineering
2 Mechanical
3 the car industry
4 military use
5 Environmental
6 pollution
7 clean up
8 solving problems
9 keen on building

4

1 h
2 f

3 a
4 d
5 b
6 e
7 c
8 g

Unit 9 Lesson 2

1

1 c
2 b
3 e
4 a

2

1 b
2 a
3 b
4 b
5 c

3

1 meteorite
2 asteroid
3 deflect
4 comet
5 devastation
6 impact
7 collision
8 threat

4

Big Thunder was opened at the Disneyland Resort in Paris.

He was first employed by Disney in 1990.

After that he was also asked to work in the aerospace industry and by the car firm Rolls Royce.

In my previous job I was always being told, 'That's not your job.'

Big Thunder ride can be enjoyed at every Disney resort in the world.

5

1 Mike Kent was employed by Rolls Royce.
2 A satellite in space is used for telecommunications.
3 I am always being told by my manager not to do other people's jobs.
4 A new attraction has been created by Disneyland.
5 Big Thunder can be enjoyed by visitors at every Disneyland in the world.
6 Four more rockets will be launched this year.
7 The planet can't be saved from a meteorite collision.
8 Our town wasn't hit by the hurricane.

6

1 be seen
2 is (was) named
3 has appeared
4 observed
5 was killed
6 was taken
7 exploded
8 was launched
9 be seen

Unit 9 Lesson 3

1

1 a
    a) a   b) a   c) an
2 an
    a) The   b) The   c) The
3 the
    a) 0   b) 0   c) 0
4 the / 0
    a) 0   b) 0   c) 0
5 the
6 0
    a) 0   b) 0   c) 0
7 the
    a) The   b) The   c) The
8 a
9 0
    a) the
10 a) The   b) 0   c) The

2

1 a
2 a
3 c
4 b
5 b
6 b
7 a
8 c
9 a
10 b

3

1 Did you see the designs I told you about? ✔
2 I went to ~~the~~ India last year. ✘
3 The Caspian Sea is the largest enclosed body of water on Earth. ✔
                 The⟋
4 ∧Weather hasn't been too good recently, has it? ✘
                                              an⟋
5 Being in a Shakespeare play is ∧ actor's dream. ✘
6 It's one of the ugliest buildings in the city. ✔
             the⟋
7 What's ∧ width of this door? ✘
8 We have a major problem with the new structure. ✔
                 the⟋
9 When does ∧ King make his speech? ✘
10 Temperatures in ~~the~~ Dubai reach over 40°C. ✘

ANSWER KEY

4

adjectives	noun
high	height
wide	width
long	length
deep	depth
square	square
circular	circle
triangular	triangle

5
1 high
2 deep
3 square
4 width
5 triangular
6 circle

6
1 three
2 72 kilometres
3 One-and-a-half times
4 The United Kingdom and France
5 52 kilometres
6 Depth
7 25 minutes
8 160 km/h
9 25 billion dollars

7a
/e/ depth, length
/ɪ/ dish, width
/iː/ ski, deep
/aɪ/ wide, high, height
/eɪ/ shape, eight

Unit 9 Lesson 4

1
1 a
2 c
3 c
4 b

3
1 I don't think that's a good idea.
   (I don't know about that.)
2 What do you think about…(What
   about…/ Why don't we…?)
3 That's a possible solution.
4 What do you think about that?
5 Great idea.
6 Why don't we ask Lance Weiss?
7 We all agree then. We'll do that.

Unit 9 Lesson 5

1
1 match
2 sections
3 make
4 cards
5 aids

6 hook
7 an impact

2
1 c
2 a
3 f
4 h
5 b
6 d
7 g
8 e

3
1 Do market research. Interview
   potential customers.
2 Build a prototype based on results.
3 Test the prototype.
4 Make any modifications and test
   again.
5 Invite journalists to the press launch.

4 (Suggested answer)
First of all you need to do some market
research. One way to do this is to
interview potential customers. Then, the
next stage is to build a prototype based
on results and test it. From the results
of that any modifications are made and
it is tested again. Finally, you invite
journalists to the press launch.

Unit 10 Lesson 1

1
1 influential
2 trendsetters
3 spread
4 must-have
5 charisma
6 imitate
7 outbreak

2a
Ooo	trendsetters, imitate, cultural
oOo	connectors, charisma, behaviour
oOoo	community
ooOo	economic, influential, epidemics

3
1 on
2 out
3 into
4 with
5 over
6 out
7 on
8 down

Unit 10 Lesson 2

1
1 Fashions and trends change at **a
   steady rate** according to research.

2 We think that a **lot of** our
   decisions about fashion are made
   independently.
3 **Plenty of** celebrities influence us and
   are copied by us.
4 The speed at which Americans buy
   albums changes a **little.**
5 **All of** the things tested for their
   popularity changed at a steady rate.

2
1 fashions
2 change
3 copy (follow)
4 innovators
5 rate
6 babies' names
7 types of dogs.

3
1 A plastic garden chair.
2 Andy Warhol wore a black leather
   jacket.
3 She looked wonderful in her white
   wedding dress.
4 James Bond often wears a black
   dinner jacket.
5 Put it in this wooden picture frame.
6 I usually just wear a pair of ordinary
   blue jeans.
7 There's a pretty red blouse in the
   window.
8 It's a silver digital watch.

4
Speaker 1: c

Speaker 2: a

Speaker 3: e

Speaker 4: f

Speaker 5: b

5
1 b
2 a
3 c
4 a
5 c
6 a
7 a
8 a

6
1 a few
2 None of
3 enough
4 plenty
5 Some
6 couple

Unit 10 Lesson 3

1a
1 Humans.
2 Women

ANSWER KEY

3 By eating well, (not being overweight), being good at dealing with stress, being optimistic, having enough money and financial security.
4 To enjoy life at present, they don't want to be old and ill.

2a
1 F
2 T
3 F
4 F
5 T
6 F
7 T
8 T

3
1 tried to live longer
2 need to find a safe place to live.
3 improving our houses and making life more comfortable
4 one person in every 10,000 who is over a hundred.
5 has been catching up to that of women's.
6 obviously smokers tend to die before
7 dealing with stress and optimistic
8 not enjoying the present / doesn't mean that you will also be healthy.

4
1 Did you say 13?
2 There's been a 40% increase.
3 I want to live until 2080. (two thousand and eighty)
4 My grandfather was born in 1915.
5 So I get this now and a hundred more next month.
6 It's fifty point one three percent less.
7 Over ten thousand telephone calls were received.
8 They think over a million people will be affected.

5
1 to live
2 to work
3 travelling
4 shopping
5 to worry/worrying
6 to pick
7 in convincing
8 to walk
9 to change
10 to buy
11 to turn up
12 to join
13 to have
14 learning
15 to see/seeing
   to stop/stopping

6
1 eating
2 having

3 walking (to walk)
4 running
5 to celebrate
6 to show
7 organising
8 to use
9 arranging
10 having

Unit 10 Lesson 4

1
1 c
2 e
3 d
4 a
5 b
6 g
7 f

Unit 10 Lesson 5

1
translation of words

word stress

parts of speech

categorise words

write a useful sentence with new words in

draw diagram or picture

3
1 e
2 d
3 b
4 f
5 a
6 c

Unit 11 Lesson 1

1
1 Reggae
2 Jazz
3 Opera
4 Horror
5 Classical
6 Science fiction
7 Animation
8 Crime
9 Soul
10 Autobiography

2
1 atmosphere
2 plot
3 chapter
4 novel
5 series
6 character

3
1 moving
2 hilarious

3 outstanding
4 groundbreaking

4
affairs	oO
country	Oo
entertainment	ooOo
computer	oOo
groundbreaking	Ooo
incomparable	oOooo

Unit 11 Lesson 2

1
1 T
2 F
3 T
4 T
5 F
6 T
7 F
8 F

2
1 g
2 e
3 d
4 c
5 f
6 a
7 b

3
1 critic
2 royalty
3 masterpiece
4 household name
5 hit
6 bestseller
7 blockbuster

4
1 he ran
2 couldn't/that day.
3 to go.
4 was going
5 had/there
6 would work/the next day.
7 was writing
8 told/to turn
9 was/that
10 her/had done

5
1 had been
2 wanted
3 'd (would) never be
4 to download
5 were enjoying
6 wanted ('d (would) like)/to star

6
1 The reporter said she was working as a model to support her family.
2 My brother said he thought it was ours/theirs.

3 Her grandchildren said they would visit her some time.
4 Rashid said they had worked on this project for three months.
5 My sister said she couldn't go to the theatre tonight/that night.

7

…why she had moved. Then she had met her first husband and it had been a very romantic time. When he had died she had been devastated. She'd thought to herself that she couldn't (wouldn't be able to) work again. So she had sold their house and had been living on her boat … She hadn't been a recluse but she hadn't wanted to meet journalists. Then one day this film script had been sent to her. She had loved the script and so she had decided to start work again.

Unit 11 Lesson 3

1a

1 g
2 b
3 e
4 f
5 c
6 a

2

M: No. I loved doing the show but I need a break.
M: No, it hasn't, though more people recognise me in the street.
M: … but last week I'd just paid for my shopping when a newspaper photographer took my picture.
M: … If I don't like it, I'll have to become a recluse, I suppose.

3

1 The journalist asked me if I I thought I would do another TV show.
2 The journalist asked me why I didn't want to do any more TV.
3 The journalist asked me if I was leaving modelling.
4 The journalist asked me how much time I spent travelling.
5 The journalist asked me how long I'd been a model.
6 The journalist asked me if I got tired of the cameras.

4

1 far and wide
2 undaunted
3 wangle
4 cover
5 chutzpah
6 convey
7 home
8 integrity

5

1 c
2 b
3 c
4 a
5 c

6

b

Unit 11 Lesson 4

1

1 Live to fight another day
2 Love in the country
3 Our dying planet
4 The mystery of Satellite 6077

High School Witches! isn't mentioned.

2a

1 very different
2 very similar
3 much better
4 less serious
5 worse than

3

Genre	Plot	Special features
thriller action romantic comedy science fiction	complex good versus evil twists and turns	stunning special effects many locations around the world superbly choreographed fight scenes

Unit 11 Lesson 5

1

Explain the purpose of your talk.

Speak clearly in a loud voice.

Structure your talk with words like Firstly, Secondly, Finally…

Tell your audience when they can ask questions.

2

1 Overall
2 Most
3 Almost
4 majority
5 whole
6 general

3 (Suggested answers)

1 On the whole, most of the audience were aged 18–45.
2 The majority of people came to the festival with their family.

3 Almost all the audience said the performers were excellent.
4 In general, people were not satisfied with the food and refreshments.

Unit 12 Lesson 1

1

1 a
2 b
3 b
4 a
5 a
6 c
7 b
8 c
9 c
10 a

2

1 arson
2 burglary
3 mugging
4 identity theft
5 forgery
6 speeding
7 murder
8 kidnapping
9 blackmail
10 hacking

Unit 12 Lesson 2

1

1 behaviour
2 circle
3 decision
4 circle
5 link / relationship
6 relationship
7 tradition
8 behaviour

2

1 would have stopped
2 would have set off
3 had happened
4 had arrived
5 hadn't had
6 might have done
7 would you have said
8 wouldn't have let

3

1 'd thought
2 hadn't chosen
3 had locked
4 might have caught
5 'd kept
6 would never have invited

5

1 I 'd've had time if I'd got up earlier.
2 They might've called earlier.

3 She wouldn't've offered if she hadn't meant it.
4 Would you've done it if you'd known?
5 We might not've passed without your help.
6 What would you've done with your life if you hadn't had children?
7 You wouldn't've wanted it any other way.
8 If he hadn't had an accident, he might've arrived at eight o'clock.

6

1 If I'd known your number…c
  If I knew your number…a
  If you have a message…b
2 We'll see you later…a
  We'd see you later…c
  We'd have seen you last night…b
3 If I had seen them…b
  If I were you…a
  If I see them…c
4 If my brother goes to a different university…c
  If my brother had gone to a different university…a
  If my brother went to a different university…b
5 We would have been on time…b
  We'll leave on time…a
  We'd be on time…c

7 Suggested answers
1 If I were you, I'd take it.
2 If I hadn't lent my friend $300, I'd be able to afford to go on holiday.
3 If you buy the car today, I'd offer you a 20% discount.
4 If you press the green button, it switches on.
5 If I'd asked her, she would have gone with me to the party.
6 If you run, you'll catch the bus.
7 If I'd studied music at University, I would have become a composer.
8 If I hadn't answered my mobile phone, I wouldn't have crashed the car into a tree.

Unit 12 Lesson 3

1
police
prosecutor
witness
bank robber

2
1 c
2 d
3 e
4 a
5 b

3

T	H	I	E	F		H	A	C	K	E	R
			I				B				
			N				A		L	K	
			G				N		A	I	
S	U	S	P	E	C	T		K		W	D
G		P	R				S		Y	N	
E		O	P					E	A		
T		L	R	A	N	S	O	M	R	P	
A		I	I						P		
W		C	N		T	H	E	F	T	E	
A		E	T						R		
Y		H	O	S	T	A	G	E			S

4
1 b
2 c
3 a
4 d

5
1 should
2 might
3 shouldn't
4 must
5 couldn't

6
1 must have
2 must have
3 can't have been
4 could have taken
5 must have been
6 should have got

Unit 12 Lesson 4

1
A 3
B 4
C 1
D 2

2
1 garage
2 Sunday
3 gun
4 give him the money
5 £2,010
6 criminal
7 relationships
8 school

3
1 facts
2 evidence
3 case
4 mind
5 minds
6 witnesses
7 jury
8 defendant
9 punishment
10 innocent

4
1 Sentence 2
2 Sentence 4
3 Sentence 10
4 Sentence 6

Unit 12 Lesson 5

1
1 Crime in the world.
2 New statistics.
3 Downward trends.
4 Robbery, burglary, car theft (street crime).
5 The world is a safer place.

2
1 crime rates
2 fallen
3 ever before
4 walk
5 fear
6 street crime
7 lowest rates
8 Denmark
9 Finland
10 overall fall
11 cases
12 Burglary
13 regarded
14 property
15 eighties
16 private homes and offices
17 security systems
18 theft
19 USA

3
1 As a result
2 so
3 As a result
4 Consequently
5 This caused
6 Because of this
7 Due to

4
1 As a result of speeding, the Government have made a new law.
2 I'm ill so I'm off work today.
3 Burglars stole some jewels. Consequently, police are looking for a green car.
4 A taxi crashed into a bus. This caused two people to be hurt.
5 Sales of the new product are poor due to the high price. (Due to the high price of the new product, sales are poor.)
6 There's very bad weather. The result is trains have been cancelled.
  As a result of very bad weather trains have been cancelled.

NOTES

NOTES

NOTES